You Are Unborn

Pointers to Your

Natural State of

Eternal Freedom

By Charlie Hayes

This book is offered with
Timeless Gratitude To

John Wheeler,

of Santa Cruz,
California, USA

Author, Teacher, and Friend.

Visit John at www.thenaturalstate.org

A few Reviews of Charlie's Books

This latest book, "You Are Unborn", is another example of the direct and unflinching message from Charlie Hayes, a "guru" who fits no molds, a "non-teacher" who doesn't wish to add to your worldly knowledge, but wants to rip all your beliefs and assumptions of separation out at the root. Charlie is a master, using metaphor and honesty, in guiding the mind towards itself, to devour itself, to recognize its own futility. And in that recognition of absence of individual self, the Being which Charlie points to may be known.

Charlie graciously gives honor to his "teachers" John Wheeler and "Sailor" Bob Adamson, while his own expression stands authentically on its own. This book contains pointing and dialogs, quotes from both modern and ancient sources, as well as the unmistakable recognition manifested in this unique, loving and hard-hitting expression known as "Charlie".

Here is an example of the crystal-clear and no-nonsense writing:

"Being is incontrovertible, inescapable and non objective; the only "separation" from Being that ever happened or could happen is in language only, and language is dreamlike, insubstantial and powerless. There is no way out of Being and no way to attain Being. To "attain" requires "don't already have" and THAT is the false identification with a movement of Divine Energy ... we call that movingness a thought ... of an "I"... which we have made solid and real in our inadvertence and ignorance; The assumption of a separate "me" is JUST an assumption."

Once again, Charlie has provided a text which can sit comfortably beside any ancient classic writing. Between the covers of this or any of Charlie's books, Truth can be found but not as we expect it, or maybe even as we might want it. Charlie clearly points out that "...no answer satisfies the mind's search because in the final Truth there IS no answer. THAT is the 'answer!'"

Charlie Hayes provides no answers, gives no crutch to hold on to, creates no foundation for the spiritual seeker. In this void of separate-self-ness, Being may be recognized but not from afar, not objectively, not as something new. In Charlie's words, "It's about the rediscovery that there is no person and yet Being Is."

Randall Friend, Author of "You Are No Thing"

"You Are Unborn" by Charlie Hayes is both a roadmap and a guidebook to the inner reality that is quite simply That which We All Really Are. It accomplishes the very difficult task of effectively using written words to point the reader into the thought and concept free essence of their very being.

It is written for all of those who sincerely seek liberation from confusion and suffering. The words flow naturally and directly from the essential heart of the author's Aware Presence in a tone and style that is both lovingly straightforward and profoundly transformative.

With a quick look at the Introduction you will find this sample:

"So this is a strange book. Rather than providing answers to the mind that are no more fulfilling than a picture of a good meal is satisfying to the body's hunger for nourishment, this book will point to the nature of the Real, and also point out the false assumptions that keep that Reality of Eternal Freedom from being known as who you are."

False identification with an assumed "me" and the thoughts and concepts that provide it with lifeless support lies at the core of human suffering. "You Are Unborn" guides us through the wasteland of our illusory, ever hungry little "me's" and into the deathless, infinite and lovingly radiant light of the pure Presence Awareness that is our true Home.

Be kind to yourself and buy, read and cherish "You Are Unborn."

John Hummell

Charlie Hayes has done it again! He points to who you really are with delicious determination! The book has many great questions from readers who are stuck in the "I" they think they are, and Charlie just absolutely destroys that belief. May truly well be the last book on non duality you may ever read. Highly recommended!!!

Alfred Paul Koegler

Charlie Hayes' latest piece of artwork is "You Are Unborn". The words come alive and present the most direct pointing to that Source that You Are.

The undying peace of your True Being is what is pointed to in this book. Charlie definitely has a style of putting into words that which cannot be put into words.

Instead of just leading the reading around in circles with a bunch of pollyanna platitudes, he cuts to the core of the matter and brings the reader face to face with Reality. Just start reading and literally lose your "self" in the pages.

If the search has had any meaning, it was to read

"You Are Unborn"; this may very well be the end of seeking!

I highly recommend getting this book, it's worth a million times the price!

JD Hazlewood, Author of "That Which Always Is"

Charlie tells it like it is and delivers the timeless message of Advaita in the tradition of Sri Nisargadatta and Bob Adamson. From the very first pages you are given the tools to know who you are and to investigate that until there are no doubts left. I am so grateful to Charlie for ... sharing his time and energy without which knowing that "I Am" would have been mere words. Through the efforts of people like Charlie, there is a growing movement in Advaita today that was first sprouted in India, cultivated in Australia and has now taken root here in America. If you are finally finished wondering when "you" will get it, read this book and end the search.

Good on ya Charlie!

Gregory LeBlanc

.... excudes love and immediate presence. If you want the feeling of actually sitting with a great teacher, but don't have access to a live teacher, this book gives you the sense Charlie is right there with you. It's much more than just reading a book.

David Trindle

Charlie Hayes has written ... on that which is the basis of all that is, and that is not. ... cuts through all the advaita jargon and gives it to you in easy to understand language. There is no-one to be enlightened there is only whatever is arising in awareness. This is the end of all searching. Read and let what is being pointed to resonate in understanding ,the egg will crack and what is there all along will be realized for no- one. Charlie thank you for giving this gift to the world.

Marc Josef

Charlie's approach is direct and clear.

The essence of you is explained in his book.

I met with Charlie, and I know he's sincere.

He's the Bob Adamson of the western hemisphere.

Michael Draper

Charlie hits an OM run. The author writes forcefully with a level of spiritual clarity that's only possible from someone with direct experience. Using quotes, dialogue and a lot of humor, Charlie relentlessly exposes how the mind gets caught up in the illusion of separation. This book is very readable, accessible and makes a significant contribution to non-dual literature. Highly recommended.

Chuck Hillig, Author of "Enlightenment for Beginners", "Looking for God, Seeing the Whole in One", "Seeds for the Soul", and " The Way IT Is".

Table Of Contents

Hello, Dear Dreamer
Wakey Wakey

~

What Is Is.
What Ain't Ain't.
And That's THIS.
And This is That
Here. Now.

~

Everyone knows, "I AM"
This I AM is the Paradise we were seeking ...
stunningly finding It already
fully present as this simple
Being-Knowing-Loving.

~

Notice right now if the
Radiant Presence behind the
"I am" - assumption
has just been overlooked.

See That Now: That is YOU.
I Am That.
You Are That.
All That Appears is That.
And That's That!
Full Stop.

Being is Knowing

Being is Knowing Without a subject "knower" or object "known". Seeing is Being, Seeing without any fixation of conceptual seer or objects seen.

This is both Knowing and Not-Knowing. Impossible to grasp, yet, IT IS.

You ARE ALREADY THIS ... Being-Awareness-Aliveness.

One Essence, One No Thing appearing to BE and BE This, As It Is..... Perfect Peace.

This is living impersonal Joy ... the Natural Eternal IS-ness.

But these are just concepts. NOT TRUE, NOT FALSE.

One Essence appearing as What IS.

Foreword:

"In 'You Are Unborn', Charlie Hayes offers a potent, lively and comprehensive presentation of the timeless, fundamental pointers of Advaita Non-duality, which is the heart-essence of the great spiritual traditions.

His 'no-holds barred', 'take no prisoners' style brings the core message of 'You Are That' into the streets.

His words and pointers, which come from his own deep investigation and direct experience, are simply infectious and contagious.

His communication is direct and uncompromising but clearly flows from a genuine love and depth of heart which is moved to take others beyond the need of further help.

Many who read this book will find their doubts and questions completely dissolved and dismantled.

In this, the joyful recognition will dawn that they are seekers no more."

John Wheeler, author of "The Light Behind Consciousness and several other books on Nondual Spirituality

Website: www.thenaturalstate.org

Introduction

Who am I? Why am I here? What is the meaning of life? What is my purpose?

Have you ever asked these questions? Most likely you have, if you have found yourself looking at this book.

The good news is that these questions have a single answer. The bad news is that the answer will not satisfy the questioner.

Rather, if this book's intent and purpose is fulfilled, the questioner himself, the seeker herself, the person asking the question, will simply fade away.

Should that happen it will probably seem like dying, but only to the "mind". But for the Self that You really are, it will simply be a welcome to the abode of Unborn Being. The Home you never really left, despite the mind's mighty dream of being separated from God, Totality, The Source.

So this is a strange book. Rather than providing answers to the mind that are no more fulfilling than a picture of a good meal is satisfying to the body's hunger for nourishment, this book will point to the nature of the Real, and also point out the false assumptions that keep that Reality of Eternal Freedom from being known as who you are.

The latter may be challenging, even threatening, to the false identity that most people wear as a mask over their naked Eternal Presence, out of fear, insecurity, arrogance, or simply, confusion and ignorance. Staying with the "conversation" can yield unpredictable insights and even a dissolution of the cloud of unknowing, so the invitation is, allow all your beliefs and cherished ideas about who and what you are to be called into question. The invitation is to leave nothing that seems to be a limit to your Original Nature remain unexamined.

To say it in a negating manner: Being Unborn, nothing is "wrong" any more ... and there never was anything "wrong".

All that is, is AS it is, eternally free, utterly open, and of the nature of a Love so vast it defies description.

May the never-born die here into the Freedom of simply being. Being Unborn, The One lives forever, appearing here and now as Life Itself. Also known as ... YOU.

Grace appeared to me as John Wheeler who provided the "knockout punch", with great and kind patience, beating the drum steadily over and over until the Final Message sank in:

The Self is No Thing. And there cannot be two No Things.

This is the meaning of "Advaita", of Nonduality. Not Two No Things. And so it is seen, by no-one ...

You Are Unborn.

With Love,
Charlie Hayes
Enid, Oklahoma, USA
January 2010

www.theeternalstate.org

non.duality@yahoo.com

+1 580.701.4793

(Note: Some pointers and dialogues are repeated through this book. It often takes more than one hammer blow to get the nail firmly imbedded, so as to pierce through the citadel of false thoughts!)

Don't Miss The Simplicity Of This

Something sees these letters and sees the forms called words, and that same ever-present something sees the space between the letters and the words, the screen of the computer that allows these to appear, and the space in which computer, body, knower, and seer, are all arising out of nowhere (now here). That Space of Being Awareness effortlessly holds and allows it all to be as it is. No resistance. Eternally Presencing Reality.

Did you overlook all these spaces and the Space-Awareness that allows it all to appear? Right here and now are you overlooking the Being-Presence that allows the seeing of the body? The observing of the I thought that appears? What is seeing? Being sees and sees the appearance of a self, reading. That Being is what You are. It takes NO time or effort to BE. This, Being-Eternally-existing, is what you are.

Don't believe the voice in your head that tells you that you are a thing that can suffer and die. Being as you are means abandoning all identities once and forever. You are That - Being, and nothing else.

Loving You,

I AM

In the Beginning...

The Christian Bible says, "In the beginning was the Word, and the Word was with God, and the Word was God."

Sounds good, right? But what they don't make clear, at least to this mind, is WHAT IS this Word which IS God? One of my Living Teachers, Sailor Bob Adamson, made this completely clear for me. In meetings with Bob in Melbourne, Australia, I heard Bob say things like "The Word is I AM", but the words are NOT the true I AM; they are only a mental translation and not the actual I AM of The Unborn Being-Awareness that you are ... and it dawned on me that THIS is what the Bible was saying, though the erroneous translations of the ancient teaching has garbled it mercilessly: this NON-conceptual I AM Bob was pointing to is GOD. And suddenly what became clear as the empty cloudless sky on a bright summer's day was, and is, YES. I AM that I AM. That, I AM, IS my true Self. Then the idea of That being something "I" possessed faded out, and what remained is the Eternal I AM, beyond all concepts of either being or not being.

Then in dialogues and a few phone conversations with Bob's student John Wheeler, it all became completely clear. In short what was seen was a knowing that had no divisions of knower and known. The "subject-object" dichotomy dissolved and the clear seeing and incontrovertible knowing was (is), YES, I Am That. That, I Am. Yes, the ancient great Word, Tat Tvam Asi, That, I Am, from the Eastern religions, and the "I Am That I Am" from the Western traditions, met and merged in an Understanding that belongs to No One (the only One there is).

That's IT. Seeing this, the seeking for wholeness ends in the obviousness that there never was any separation form Source or God in Reality. The dream ends and awakening has happened ... to no one. The final truth is just this: I Am That, You Are That, and All of This, is That.

And That's THAT.

That

That "I" or "me" thought comes and goes. What does NOT change? What does NOT come or go? Pure Awareness.

All these thoughts appear. In what? The serene ever-peaceful presence-awareness that is unchanging. Ever fresh and always the reality prior to any appearance. No matter what appears, that awareness is here first and always ... never missing. Is there anything "missing" for awareness itself? Become aware of awareness ... notice that without awareness NOTHING can appear. No thought can appear unless you are aware! Look carefully at this: is there anything missing or wrong with that awareness itself? Notice this awareness. Put "the attention" directly on this aware presence. You are that. And That's That.

Being Living Freedom ... The Natural State

Being is knowing, without the false assumption of a person which, in direct practical experience through a cogent investigation, cannot be found. So it boils down to this: There is NO person to attain any state, no special state to attain; the whole thing was a myth; and dispelling the myth is no more complex than getting real about what IS TRUE... knowing the Truth of what you are and refusing any compromise the mind wants to use to paste some imagined limitation onto that Timeless Awareness.

Realizing that the "I" is a CONCEPT with NO ACTUAL reality, and that "time" is ONLY another mental concept, pulls the plug on the illusion once and for good. Looking directly at what IS from/AS Naked Awareness, which is the necessary and ever-clear and present backdrop for ALL experiences, and seeing directly the Source of the "I Am", the freedom you are comes naturally back to the foreground. And life goes on in effortless joy and there is as Nisargadatta put it, "nothing wrong any more." Seeing that ALL ideas of who or what we are *are* absolutely FALSE, the deal is done.

So in the end it is as it is before the beginning: You Are Unborn. Absolute freedom. The natural, or Eternal, Being-That-You-Are! As the sages like Sri Nisargadatta have pointed out, it all comes down to knowing that what you are is non-conceptual-izable. That keeps it basic and simple.

Ponder this: Seeking "Wholeness, Completion, Happiness, Love or "Liberation" from "Another", whether that "revered other" be a "Guru, Guide, Lover, or Friend", is a perfect way to avoid Paradise. Paradise is THIS. Just as it Is and just as it Isn't.

All seeking "out there" is a dream of a "me", foolishly knocking on the door to Paradise, from inside Paradise. Paradise is only lost in seeking it. This Loving Oneness Cannot Be Known.

To "know" Oneness there would have to be a sense of separation FROM Oneness. Who cannot see the fault in that logic?

The Eternal State is Being. . .

There Is Only Being...

Being Is One Knowingness ...

YOU Are This One, Unborn, Eternal Being

The Nondual Knower *Of* This Knowingness.

Before God Is, You Are

The true I … I AM… is universal and impersonal…

Q: This might sound crazy but somewhere I know that I am missing Life itself by not allowing this knowledge to be fully present and totally lived ... this is the main suffering... how can one stop pushing Life away when seen that this is what is happening?

C: All those words, all your questions, are intrinsically meaningless thoughts. Notice the unchanging I AM that they appear in. All that is temporal (temporary!). What never changes is what you are. That is Love, accepting all that appears on its own Face, the presence of awareness that IS right here right now. Just see what is fully alive, present... and knowing right now, right here, before 'time', ('your name'), or 'charlie' concepts appear. You are That which cannot be touched by any word or object. That is what we call being-knowing-love. Remember NO word is the actual! The word love is not Love. Love is WORDLESS yet lovingly allows any and all words, objects, appearances ... without judgment, unaffected ... as the Gita pointed out, That cannot be blown by wind, wetted by rain, burnt by fire. To know yourself as that requires the courage to give up all identification... all identities are false...reality is identity-less ... give up all ideas such as "I am this body with this name".

Know this for yourself, here and now: "Before God is, I AM."

Ask this also, who precisely IS this "I" that is "missing life itself by not allowing... etc" ... where is that separate I and is it actually a real thing apart? All the while you are claiming to be missing life, life is happening! Who cannot see this? There is nothing in the way of Life. If you believe you can alter anything in this dream of being in life itself then stop the next hurricane from hitting Florida! It is our arrogance that claims we can "not allow" anything including realization that we are life itself. Drop it like the hot knife it is that seemingly murders your aliveness right now. All you have to lose is everything you hold dear... your imaginary limited self. Losing everything, the Paradise you never lost is "regained".

Q: To keep on pondering the jewels you gave here is what I feel is right as to respect their deep value...by now in investigation, no one is found as ever present I and at the same time I AM HERE...Who and where? No answer can actually fulfill the question ... so the only thing that remains is the sense of being and the looking ... Meet you in Paradise ... Love To You in Freedom.

C: You say, "no one is found as ever present I and at the same time I AM HERE ..." that is the key insight! What is that I which is here now? The I Consciousness (A'Ham) ... endless beginningless Being. THAT I AM is true reality and love. Notice that THIS I AM is NOT a concept, NOT an idea, NOT even an experience! This I AM is the Paradise we were seeking ... stunningly finding It already fully present as this simple Being-Knowing-Loving. So you have rediscovered Paradise in the simple seeing "there is no separate I", and at the same eternal-time, the Infinite I AM. Here and now that I AM endures forever. You carry the whole universe here, in your own heart! So I say welcome back to the Home you never left (the mind lied but now you know that Truth that sets us free in Itself. YAY!)

Another way to point ... the True I IS Ever-Present, Always ON ... in the same way that even when it appears to be dark outside we KNOW that the sun is ever-present, shining despite the appearance that it is not because the earth blocks the physical eye's view of it ... the knowing is naturally, the earth revolves around the sun and it is never not... Read More shining. In this way see that the Light of Being, Awareness-Light, IS always shining and cannot be extinguished despite the appearance of thoughts, ideas and false beliefs that like the earth seems to keep the sun from view seem to keep the Light of the Eternal I from view. YOU are that Pure I that is seen here now, and That is the Self of All. Know this now, don't refuse to be That, and don't pretend ever again you are not That. That, I AM. There is but ONE I-I BEING the knowing I AM. This is the truth (satyam).

What Fuels The Seeking?

Q: The seeking/suffering here has seemed to intensify as of lately. I feel naked if I'm not always investigating or reading some non dual passage at least a few times or more daily. I got to go see Unmani Liza Hyde in person a few months ago, she was really great and i also enjoyed the Podcasts you and Scott Kiloby had with her also. Thoughts are always coming up why after looking at non duality after all this time seeking/suffering is still continuing... Much Love and good health to you

C: So ... that is what is happening. Now look at what FUELS that ... what is that which energizes the body, the thoughts, the feelings, perceptions, emotions .... What powers the seeking, the entire happening of whatever is appearing right here, right now? There IS Energy. There IS a source of all movement. Look for that source, starting from Here and looking UNDER what shows up ... rather than telling the story, find that which provides the energy FOR the story. In short start HERE. Look HERE. What gives the life it's life-ing here now? Always here always now, there IS Energy-Aliveness. Put the focus on that Energy, that race of Being-alive. Keep it simple. Telling a story over and over makes no impact ... where going UNDER the story can. See how that goes and stay in touch, my friend.

"There is no 'out there' out there".

The Nature of This

Once the seeing happens that "I Am" is known as the Natural Eternal Truth, then whatever appears in this space-like being-awareness is naturally and effortlessly left as it is ... unmodified, unaltered, uncorrected.

That is acceptance of what IS with no false belief in any ideas that may be arising in spacelike awareness of an acceptor of a thing accepted.

It Is. That is the Eternal Seeing-Being, naturally embracing all that appears.

This is Love ... not the absence of hatred or the presence of love in the relative way, but Absolute Love and only That.

And ...

Although in Truth there is no seeker, no path, no attainment, no teacher, no realization: If there is seeking happening then this may resonate.

Perhaps the habit is to identify your self as the thought "I" ... as in "I Am". Notice right now if the Presence behind the I thought has been overlooked.

Break into the habit, being aware of That Presence as your True Identity. This takes no time nor practice. It's just a natural seeing, right here, right now. And that's the end of seeking; the Natural, Eternal State has been found to be never missing. There is no mystery to this. It is, simply, what you already always ARE. Right Here Right Now You Are This. In This, There IS No End and No Beginning.

Can The Inquiry 'Who Am I' Really Work?

Q: I for some reason am still just attracted to 'the spiritual stuff' and like always want to just read a short pointer or so. I came across your newest video which is basically 'Who Am I?' and to drop all questions but this. Then all today from work to commute to school to back home I was asking Who Am I? It was pretty easy for the first half a day because it was more of a mantra then a real investigation except at some moments. Then on the way home I really began to listen for an answer or try to find this 'me' and I realized that there really is nothing that comes up when the question is asked and I don't know who I am....and then this piece of shit fear came back again. I began to wonder how easily all the good feelings I've been feeling these past days didn't belong to me because I couldn't find this me I was attributing these feelings to.

C: That's consistent with the knowing-seeing of the absence of a "person", that false entity has been uncovered, by no one at all! It's a paradox.

Q: I then realized that we at the core love ourselves more than anything else.

C: Sounds good! Now let us be really clear … ask you, who realized? There is no-one to realize, or not … such claims are just divine infinite-energy-pulses of noises in a brain-machine … noises that have NO intrinsic meaning at all. An aftereffect of clear nonconceptual absence may well arise as an experiencing of love and peace, and then in some cases, the thought I returns from nowhere attempting to CLAIM this "insight-knowing" for a "knower", a false concept added to the false person. Some have called this happening a "flip-flop". No problem; it passes on its own. No need to resist or try to fix that; simply keep looking for what the sound in the brain calls "me". As John Greven says; "What the One source is - cannot be perceived or conceived simply because there is no other to perceive the One. Yet, there is an undeniable presence that the "I" thought refers to. Find what the mind calls "I." Be relentless until the Source is clear. Everything conceivable and perceivable is appearance - in the presence/awareness - that belongs to no one. That, I am."

And THAT, YOU ARE.

The knowing is a functional aspect of this Presence-Awareness that you are. The knower is a powerless meaningless IDEA and nothing more. Ask yourself, can a thought actually DO anything at all? No. There is NO control center where you can make or avoid desirable or undesirable appearances in this living waking dream-life…. And, all the while time, space, sensations, thoughts, feelings come and go in YOU … the Existingness-Presencing-Peace that is the Unchanging invincible nakedness of nothing and everything … the Not-Two of Eternal Presence. The world of forms, body appearances, stars, suns, all of it, is one Energy-Being, showing out in a projection of that Consciousness-Intelligence that is more magical that any imagination could hold, creating and uncreating itself in a timeless strobe like spontaneous and uncaused play of Love-Light… speaking only poetically as That is beyond any description, experience or grasping. That is always forever Just Here.

Q: God bless you my brother. I never knew that what we were looking for was here the whole time. It is this love that lets everything arise the good and bad. Funny thing is that life just goes on I don't feel like I'm in a state where suffering cannot occur which what I thought all this would lead too. I still do the things I do but realize it's not that serious. I have done inquiry for the last 2 months but I never forgot and maybe it was operating in the background but who knows. Anyways I'm just so glad that there are people like you that are living and patiently reminding us of that of which we never lost. God bless you take care my friend. PS: It's effortless now, what the hell did I ever have to do!?

C: Great! Welcome back to the Home you never left!

All There Is, Is Nothing, Being "The Show"

Q: The last few weeks have been tough, anxiety felt like it was gonna blow me up and I didn't know what to do. But then I realized that when I read your material all I did was read without actually 'looking'. I have this habit of wanting to just finish anything I start reading.

C: Lots of people have that one ... to rush forward without really stopping to look where the pointers point. Good catch!

Q: So I went back to "Paradise Found" and read slowly, and in the last few days there seems to be a difference, I don't know what it actually is but I've started to do things that I used to find near impossible, like getting out of bed....LOL!

C: The pendulum swings both ways, from lethargy to energy, sickness to health etc. Now what is that which never changes, that IN which the pendulum swings? THAT is what is continually pointed to as the Reality that allows for the entire appearance to appear, the unmanifest to manifest, the Absolute to appear as the relative.

Q: When there are anxious feelings I now automatically ask, 'who's anxious?', 'Where is the 'I' or 'me' that says it feels anxious?', 'who is it that is asking these questions?' - No answer - Who, who , who, who , who, who, & where - show yourself - no answer!

C: THAT is what you are – no-answer, no-thing, there is no personal entity doing anything; there is the direct seeing that yes, there is no me, and yet, I AM. Just That: I AM and prior to language.

Q: When there are no thoughts, then sometimes images will pop up or subtle feelings but they all come & go - without thoughts, images, & feelings - what is there? - is there anything?

C: There is Nothing. There is Everything. Absolute appearing as Relative. Being. Awareness-Consciousness. Aliveness. THAT beating a heart and growing hair 24/7 until the organism disintegrates. No one was born. THIS – Birthless and Deathless, One No Thing essence appearing as all that arises – a quiet wow.

Q: One pointer that felt like how a Mike Tyson punch would probably feel like was your pointer to question: What is prior to language? When we were all babies we knew no languages, we couldn't talk, there was no 'I' or 'me', yet the body didn't die - it still functioned perfectly! - So how did that happen? Is there perhaps something other than 'I' or 'me' that is actually the godfather undercover?

C: There is ONLY non-seperate Being, being nothing, being something, being everything. NOT two. No mommies and daddies in the background taking care of us or pulling the strings. There is NO such thing as a "Father-Mother-God" apart from a language of dualism that assumes "I am me" and "There are others", and "a Big Dude named God" running this show. ALL there is is The Show. AKA EVERYTHING.

Q: Many thanks for your pointers, emails, & website - thank you, much love.

C: It's my pleasure. Much Love right back atcha, "me called not me". One I AM, appearing as many. The magic show! Enjoy!

The Energy And Nucleus Of Suffering

Q: I have been watching some of your clips on YouTube and reading some on your blog. And I have a question: A couple of months ago "I" had this experience of how my true identity was not me as a person. There was just this nothingness and the one I thought was me was just seen as an illusory identity. Like a software program in this mind/body-mechanism to make it able to function in this physical dimension. But this mechanism had no identity, because, well, it's just a mechanism. Instead there was NO me at all. NO identity. Or you could also say that "my" identity was a vast nothingness. I'm not really a person.

C: Exactly. That is the core insight... the aware and present seeing-knowing that yes, there is no person, and that seeing IS the timeless reality. Now, however, you say "there WAS no person". There still IS no person, and there never was or could be a real separate "person"; that was and is only a false assumption taken on board as an identity that never was more than a mirage, an illusion. But that is ONLY a concept and NO concept is "true"!

Moreover, the idea "there WAS no person' is just a presently arising thought in unchanging naked awareness. You ARE that Naked Awareness. No idea or concept is the Real You. Even to say "You are Naked Awareness" is in a way, false; or only a pointer. The word is NOT the actual.

Q: And to come to my question; after this it has been problematic to find the so called "meaning" with anything. Somehow I can't see the point in anything. Meaning with life? ... I can't see any such thing. So what if someone becomes "realized", "enlightened" or whatever? (I don't see how anyone can BECOME something because it seems we are just eternal awareness/consciousness anyway.)

C: Quite right, my friend. But remember that the concept awareness/consciousness is not the actual space-like essence at all. NO word can capture what is essentially wordless, yet paradoxically, filled with energy and a very alive presence.

"Form is emptiness, emptiness is form" is a good pointer: These are NOT TWO. This is Non-Duality.

Q: The concept of "meaning" just doesn't stick to anything anymore. This nothingness seems to be "stuck" in every aspect of my life.

C: Whose life!? This is a reinforcement of the false ... the return of an assumption held onto that there actually IS a "person" ... and now that "person" claims "there is no person". That's why the pointer "there is no person" really does not get at what we need to get at ... the assumption itself, the pre-verbal "knowing I am me" that is still operating here. Your sharing shows that this false assumption is still operating "in deep background", and it is *that* which needs to be challenged, uprooted, and found to be unreal.

Q: Suddenly everything is nothing. Even emotions. My emotions seem almost numb somehow. Everything is no neural and in a way very dull.

C: Yes, that can happen so long as that assumption referenced above remains fundamentally and directly unchallenged.

As John Wheeler reminded me repeatedly, "Understanding is the key." Understanding comes from investigation. Get really curious to see what this I is that claims "there's no meaning" or "it's all empty and numb somehow". That is "the end game". Get down to brass tacks: what IS this assumed sense of life, sense of being, that still operates as a seemingly separate me-person despite the insight that happened? A concept, the "I thought", is just another learned idea. And it's not there in deep sleep, yet the livingness goes on just fine without it. Right?

Yesterday's insight has no value at all; it's dead conceptualizing now. Presently, what is real? Your Being Itself.

That Being remains forever Unborn. No thing yet appearing as everything. To paraphrase Sri Nisargadatta, when the seeing "I am no one" happens, there arises wisdom. But that is only half of this. When the seeing is "I am everything, everyone", there arises Love. And this Love is the Reality of your very Being.

Which Nisargadatta expressed as, "My silence sings. My emptiness is full". So the invitation is to get very, very interested in what it is that "feels numb" and asserts "there is no one". If there is truly no one who would be making these claims of some lack or limitation, some apparent suffering? The false nexus of suffering ... that pre-verbal assumption of a "me" ... simply cannot stand up to solid, earnest investigation. At ANY moment of suffering, stop and LOOK ... see what is really happening. You will find thoughts arising in your own aware presence, and a sense of personhood that fixes the thoughts to itself and kind of "knows" (incorrectly), that "this is me and about me." And that is the root of the root of the whole thing, the nucleus. Pull out the energy of belief from the assumed identity and the system collapses. And life is lived in freedom and profound peace. That's worth going for, isn't it?

So: This is the kind of guidance I got from John Wheeler. Now it's passed on to you, with love. The ball is in your court now, my friend. Please feel free to write again as the One moves that to arise and happen. Meanwhile, BE. Just BE what you already ARE, Naked Unborn Awareness ... and only That.

Seeing into the manifestation with and from Bare Naked Awareness, find out of that assumed sense-of-me is real once and for all. Thanks for a good question.

Who Do You Think You Are?

Are you really separate from me, other, god, world, now, brother, earth, mother, sky, I, emptiness, form, nothing, energy, silence, sound, stillness, movement, anything, or everything? What are You Really? Is that clear? Obvious? Or NOT? Have a good look.

Q: The one thing that feels real is this energetic feeling that I am here and am in the body. Forgetting all words apart from, "I feel here in this body." There is a soreness around the heart area...I feel constricted. Tight in this body.

C: So that is what is happening now. And all the while the Essence that You ARE remains as shining stillness, the No Thing that appears as everything. And what exactly is everything you wrote above made of? Language. Thoughts. The ONLY problem, in my view, is that you believe thoughts to be real, true, and who you are, and that they are also ABOUT who you are. But these thoughts are NOT the Reality of Being!

There is this very popular myth that there is a possibility for a person, a "me", to get enlightened. Someday, of course; never just NOW!

There IS NO attainment "for the me". You cannot "get it" ever. No way. Why? Because this No Thing is already what you are. And That is no person; no fictional entity can attain its own absence!

Can No thing locate No Thing? Where? When? How?

This No Thing is appearing AS everything. All the energy-patterns we label as "things", "time", "location" etc. are ALL That. And, everything includes, well, everything! Right?

Awareness IS. Content APPEARS. Yet Awareness and Content are Not Two.

This Cognizing Self- Shining Self-Aware No Thing is the very seeing which IS happening here. Now.

There is the seeing of these marks on your computer screen or on the blank pages of this book; there is the breath happening, hearing of sounds is happening, now notice that this all happens without your needing to take charge; all perceptions are all happening while the perceiving witnessing Self-Aware Emptiness "watches" ... it is unimaginable, the mind cannot grasp this ever because the mind is a thing and YOU are NO Thing ... that's really all there is to this.

Look into this: Can something come from no Thing?

Impossible! So ALL there is, is No Thing, one essence, one Energy, one Nondual Knowing-Beingness. One Without A Second.

Not Two.

Notice this also: You cannot NOT BE. Being is indisputable. Inescapable. Yet Being is not what you think it is.

We call that Being, "I AM". That ... I AM ... IS this No Thing. The word I is NOT the True I of Being-Awareness. The word "Am" is NOT the Timeless Nonconceptual Isness.

Sit with this, and notice that whatever is happening in the appearance of things, that No Thing is always so, always "ON". That's it. Seeing That as That is the key. It is not the mind; mind is thoughts appearing IN That.

Don't make these words into some new nondual "religion" though. These are only pointers. There is NO answer. That is the final answer. For NO ONE.

Tiredness appears. But who is tired? A body has tiredness. Is that owned by any "me" identity? No. That is just a story we believed in our ignorance, ignoring Awareness and identifying as the wordplay of the deluded mind... Are you that? No. You are the Aware Being that recognizes the content of Awareness. Don't identify as content; drop back to the Beingness, awake, aware, never absent. That is what you are. You cannot get it ... You ARE IT. Understand that the always on presence awareness that sees and knows these words and spaces IS what is sought.

ALL of your mental doubts and confusion can be resolved but

you have got to do the work. That is the bad news! It's up to YOU to investigate, is this "me" with a "sense of contractedness" actually REAL? Or is that just a believed thought-story ...the "tale filled with sound and fury, signifying nothing", with no real substance? Like stormy weather in a clear empty sky, you are the Unborn Being which registers and allows whilst remaining untouched by the stormy weather. The mind is stormy or calm, depending on its programming and the programmed stimulus-responses in the world appearance. Does that touch the real You? No.

And don't use the "Nonduality Dogma Cop-out" of "There is no person so who must do any work?" That is a half-assed approach! The you that you still believe you are (as evidenced by your messages) ... that is who must get down to brass tacks. So DO it.

Seeking seems to produce suffering, doesn't it? We seek and never find what we seek? And that leads to frustration? That is what happened here. The suffering seemed to me to be a description of a real phenomenon, called ... MY life, MY circumstances, and it was all about me. That sense of being a me in a body in a world was so ingrained, I was blind to the possibility that it was not real. So I would read and seek and yak with people I had on some pedestal who I figured knew the real story while poor me, I am just this idiot who can't get it so there must be a flaw ... in ME.

What was not being looked into was, a) what is suffering? And b) what is "suffering" made of? What is the constitutive element, the glue of it?

Some clues:

Bob Adamson has said, "What's wrong with right now, if you don't think about it?" James Allen has said, "As a man thinks, so he becomes". Descartes has said, "I think therefore I am". What are all these guys pointing to? Thoughts.

It may well seem that thought is describing, not creating. But what if that is ass backwards? What if the suffering is a

PRODUCT of our deeply believed thoughts and not a description of some actual real thing? Have you looked at suffering in that way?

Mount good challenges to that cherished belief that there really IS a "person" and there really IS a world which the person lives in and life really IS lousy for the person and so on. But what if "the person" is ONLY thoughts? A story believed incorrectly? And what if the suffering is NOT a description of a real set of "my circumstances" but only a created set of fundamental unchallenged beliefs? The quick answers won't do. Digging deep into these questions may reveal that there is but ONE fundamental misconception that acts as the "glue" for the false assumptions that life really IS this way, for "me" ... the idea, believed, I AM ME.

The idea! The very idea, "I am me", is what? Thought. Nothing more. The notion "I am me and no one can tell me otherwise!" is so fundamental and so deeply believed that it no longer occurs as a thought, but rather "who I am". "I think therefore I am".

But LOOK: Can a passing "IDEA" have any power to do or cause anything? No. Seeing that pulls the plug on the whole illusion.

Look at it: It's all just ideation, meaningless mental chatter.

"I think I am me, and don't see that I think that, so I suffer". So it becomes invisible ... the mind has cleverly hidden that thought away so as to not allow any challenge to its validity! So the lie is now the truth. I am, I am me, and that me suffers. Because that me has made a decision, that one kind of experience is better than another, and wants only the nice experiences and resists the not so nice experiences. All because of one core mistake ... the assumption that a thought is what I am. "As a man thinketh...so he becomes....."

It seemed to me that the energy-contraction or the emotional movement came first and the thought was reporting in that, but John Wheeler pointed out to me that my "experience" was, quite simply, NOT the truth of what is real ... and that the being-contraction arises in language at the core. The simple test for this is, in deep sleep, there is no suffering because there is no thought. In the waking state, the thought of a separate person kicks in, and since it has been believed for a good long while, and the whole world is in agreement that there are individual persons, it basically goes unchallenged. The work is to look at this really deeply; it is not hard, but needs a simply curiosity to look into what is happening when there is suffering going on and trace that suffering back to locate the actual source. Rather than take on some set of spiritual beliefs about what is possible or not, who we are or not, or believe any description to be the reality, get down under the appearance of suffering, such as frustration, anger, unwanted tiredness etc and get to the true root of that which says, "This ain't IT", "I don't get it" etc.

It seems to take some courage to do this, and I encourage you to face the fact that all suffering is born ONLY in language, in other words in thought, that as John pointed out to me the thoughts of suffering IS the source and cause of itself, and imbedded under those thoughts is the core belief–thought "I am me". And that belief in a "me" is the root of the root! That "I am ME" thought (THOUGHT!) is, in these cases of suffering, essentially adding the judgment, the assertion-complaint, "and this sucks".

And so the thoughts go on reinforcing the false while the truth remains hidden away ... until it is directly challenged "in open court".

Don't be fooled by beliefs and concepts that reinforce the notion of a faulty, separate individual with a name and form. To repeat the simplest and most potent pointer from Bob Adamson, "what is wrong with right NOW unless you think about it"?

Those who are living in this natural state, "being lived", doer-less, me-less, are sharing what works, without an agenda, without making a big deal about it, without endless retreats, without any sales pitch, and are generously offering you what works. It's up to you to take it and work with it. This is how John Wheeler helped me see what the nature and the source of suffering really IS ... and gently encouraged me to look for myself. I encourage you in the same way.

Feel free to call or write if you like. Meanwhile, in any moment where there is suffering ... i.e. frustration, resignation, or an upset to the mental well being of any sort, look into the happening of it in that very moment and trace what is happening back ... you will find it is all thought, and believing the thought of "being me" is really the only issue, the only lie to be rooted out and discarded.

Don't believe the mind. And don't look to the mind. The mind is the wrong tool for the job; you cannot "think your way out" of the mind's delusion.

Get down to the core! Who are you? Who? Do you exist? Are you separate from me and the world in truth? No. Rediscovering this, suffering is done and over. Go for that!

(Follow-up)

Q: Thanks. I have read your email a few times. Thank you for the book also..... [a free version of Paradise Found, available on request]. One thing that those who appear to me to be liberated or living from true nature or whatever is the correct way of saying it, is your unconditional generosity. It's a common trait. And thank you for that.

C: My pleasure, my friend. As to generosity, I appreciate the kind words, and, that happening is a real surprise to me! This machine called Charlie was very UN-generous and selfish for most of its apparent life! But something shifted after meeting and talking this out with John Wheeler. I am just as thankful for that as anyone!

Q: Some who I have been to see a few times would say that there is no you that you can do any work. Who is going to do the work they would say?

C: The straight answer is simple: YOU already ARE what is sought and missing that is a function of accepting a false assertion as true. That is why investigation is almost always required, though clear seeing and knowing the truth of what you are certainly can arise in any fashion and there are no rules. But this is for the "you" you think and believe you are ... falsely!

Who must do the work is that one YOU still think and believe you are; the limited "me" that you apparently "know your self to be".

I cannot stress too strongly how often I hear this. And I went through exactly the same confusion! I heard it said by various people who talk about this that "there IS no person, there is nothing to do because there IS no one so who indeed would or could do any investigation..." etc.

The problem is that the mind hears that, it sounds good, so it takes that pointer on as some real truth. But NO pointer, no matter how sharp or clear, is TRUE. Words are ONLY pointers, and to believe a pointer and get all resigned and in despair because so and so says there is no one, is a game the mind plays to keep surviving ... and survival of the entity-belief is suffering.

Believe nothing. This is NOT a matter of belief, assertion, or comprehension! Leave no stone unturned in the investigation. The point is, rather than take anyone's word for this, to really look for yourself, see for yourself. Most "teachings" start out with the notion that you ARE a separate flawed person, an entity, call it a contraction or whatever, but what we share here is to reject all such notions and beliefs, no matter how true or authentic they sound, and LOOK. Stop. Look. See if this proposed "contracted entity" has an actual substance and any actual "independent nature" whatsoever. The classic pointer urges the seeker to stop and ask the mind to come up with an answer to the question "Who Am I"? Until the mind simply collapses. And the "one asking" is the "you" that YOU are still claiming in various ways to be "you", and we say put that believed-in-you to the task of finding out, "Who am I?" Who???

How some folks can assert that true sages, such as Ramana Maharshi or Sri Nisargadatta, "had it wrong" somehow, shows a real arrogance as far as I am concerned. The sages said, investigate! Look into this sense of being a separate self and see if it is really true, or merely an ignorant assumption taken to be true ... and as Bob Adamson told me, the false simply cannot stand up to investigation.

So don't believe these things that are said as pointers, NOT truths. No matter how strongly the assertion is made, to merely accept an assertion like "there is no one" to be some nonduality "gospel" is a huge mistake, my friend.

Q: Though in saying that I do still believe thoughts like you said. I still believe that they are me... I must. I do see more and more though that they are nothing more than an appearance.

Another teacher said to me once that all there is, is thinking. Does that mean just that thinking arises in the same way breathing does in the same way a sound of a lawn mower outside arises but they don't arise to anybody?

C: Yes. Thought are happening. WHO thinks them? Observe thinking happening and ask, WHO is thinking? Where is the thinker? You will find only space. No Thing. And that, No Thing, is your true Self. Not the CONCEPT No Thing, the REAL No Thing that is unconcealed in the asking "Who Am I? And finding no answer, no self, and no separation.

Look! Are you aware? Yes. Is there anything wrong with that awareness? NO. Do NOT believe or accept or deny anything. LOOK.

Q: So does this mean that what I am is as much the sound of the lawnmower as a thought or as breathing. But it just so happens that I believe I am my thoughts and exclude all else...

C: THAT is the ignorance that keeps one suffering.

Q: The hardest thing in some ways is expectation; i.e. no matter what book I have read there is talking about some sort of a wonderful experience... But maybe I look for that. One guy says the mind can only see carrots [imagined states to gain] ... so like you said I am waiting for something that will happen. It's never now..... This is never enough.... And these are all just thoughts.

But they feel claustrophobic sometimes like there is nothing but thought. Isn't belief just another thought? And isn't not-believing just another thought?

C: Belief and non-belief are certainly thoughts. The question is WHO or what is this assumed "believer"? Is there one? NO. But what you ARE is NOT ANY thought. This Space-Like Awareness that you are is clear and present at all times whether there are thoughts, beliefs, no beliefs etc, or not. THAT is BEYOND belief and non-belief; beyond knowing and not knowing. Impossible to grasp and yet Solid and Real.

And totally FREE. Absolute Being, One without a second … The One Thou Art.

The only issue is that we, until there is a pointing that is heard, accept the false to be true and the true to be false. Reverse it!

My friend, you say a lot of stuff as if you are reporting some "truth". But WHO SEZ? Find out: IS there a thinker and an experiencer? Who Am I? Who asks who am I? Does Presence Now have anything wrong? What is wrong with right now? Unless I believe thoughts to be my self? WHO AM I? Ask that believed-self called "you" (your sense of being, the false assumption "I am me"), until there is no one left to ask. There will be no answer that will ever satisfy you. Only the question matters, NOT any answer which would just be more concepts, more false identity-thought.

Just do it. No belief and no pointer will get the job done. YOU yourself must get down to it. But START from the one FACT you DO know for absolute certain: The knowing of your very Being.

You ARE: There IS Presence, Awareness, Consciousness, but THAT is NOT a thought the mind can grasp. Being IS, Eternal and Unborn. Here and Now. And You are That.

THAT is a conscious Presence that is aware of anything that appears and remains untouched by anything that appears. That Thou Art. There is ONLY That.

At first it may seem that the inquiry leaves a sense of emptiness, a sense of detachment. While not the "Final Seeing", that "state" is a great opening to the Unborn Reality that You are. The ancient sages called it Viveka (Discrimination) and Vairagya (Dispassion). The gate, my friend. Open the gate!

Being that, no thing, abiding as that no thing, with no attempt to fix or change that, naturally leads to the obverse... no thing is rediscovered as being everything. But to try to leap over the false self center and failing to get down under that false self with good solid investigation, by simply accepting some teacher's assertion to be true, is a common mistake in this search.

So let's nail it down! YOU are UNBORN. Being, just That and nothing else. Full Stop.

If there is any doubt, confusion, or delusion left after you ponder and work this, please schedule a consultation. Only so much can be done on e-mail. Obviously you have already invested a great amount of time and money in going to see teachers, buying all the books, etc. why not end this once and for good? If the consultation doesn't work don't offer any donation! But we will need to do this on Skype or you'll need to call me. I cannot afford to pay for overseas calls when there is no compensation. It's just a matter of practicality in the appearance of things as I feel sure you can understand. Be well (in fact, JUST BE!) and stay in touch as needed. Like I said let's get this nailed down for you.

Q: (Later) ... For a moment there I had a feeling I was everything in this room and I couldn't find myself anywhere.

C: That is what you are. NO thing, no location.

Q: And then I am trying to get that feeling back; so I ask myself, "who is trying to get that feeling back?" and I can't answer that.

C: Unknowing! That is the solvent ... BE with that NO Answer! Being with not knowing! So keep looking ... if the "me" comes back so to say, ask WHO is expecting either an answer or no answer! Let the mind fully collapse. That is the essence of it.

What Is, IS … Or Is It?

Q: Sometimes I realize I exist (not the conceptual I) and in those moments things are sweet and nice and what is, is! It's like waking up to a beautiful dawn (of course there is no one to wake up). However, suddenly there is suffering and I am back to the little I being ME. I am back to seeking, etc.

C: But where IS this I"? In deep sleep "you" are not there, yet the life of that organism lives without your being there at all. The exact same is happening in the waking and dreaming states, with the trivial exception of a thought coming and going, which out of insecurity or fear we attach to and identify with. That "I" thought DOES represent something. What does that "I" point to? Undeniably, YOU ARE and prior to any thought, that Existingness IS. It's the most obvious clarity. Overlooking that in favor of a thought story of a fictional "I" is the cause of all suffering.

Q: I have been baffled as to how you do self inquiry. I know you can ask, 'who am I' but I still am unsure if it's an intellectual question or if it's something to drop into presence during still moments. After reading the chapter on, 'how do I do self inquiry' in your book 'Paradise Found'. I asked myself, 'who's asking' and then tried going deeper but I come down to being just IT or the BRAIN. This is where I get stuck. There is the sense that I am the brain and operating consciously from that and observing its thinking. Any ideas?

C: Read your own message again. Watch your own mind go I-I-I-I-I-I! Listen to your story of an "imaginary bound-up identity" and look right now: Is it real? Or is it a THOUGHT? Can a thought do anything? That "I" cannot really do self inquiry! How could a thought find it is not real? It's tail chasing. Where is an "it" or a "brain" without words, concepts? All of which just come and go in Infinite Awareness, which you cannot "know" because you ARE That...

Settle in with the pointers rather than try to "do" your way out. There is ultimately NO way out for a "you" that is unreal to start with! That said, if some inquiry or whatever comes up by itself, fine. This is not about rejecting practice, nor about the "I" understanding its true nature. The "I" doesn't HAVE a "true nature"!

Again WHERE is this separate entity with the label "I" that "gets stuck"?

There is no one in there so who would "do" some "practice"? Look at this: When you assume that what you are is a limited finite person, which you represent in language as "I", or "me", you reinforce that assumed identity by taking up this or that practice to perfect this finite persona. But if that practice assumes you are a separate identity, how could that practice allow you to transcend that false persona? That is like turning the dirty cop in the precinct out to catch the dirty cop in the precinct. And yet it appears to happen. That's the paradox of this, which the mind cannot ever grasp because the "mind" is only a thought! Can a thought grasp thought?

Q: Also, I have been thinking of meeting you. I know you live far away (I am in MD) and was wondering if it is possible to meet you in person some day?

C: You are welcome to come any time. However there may be no particular advantage in a face to face ... I found on meeting John Wheeler that his writings were actually more potent in a way owing to the absence of perceptive distractions! Same for our phone talks wherein he set it all straight in relatively short order, ending a three decades long search that, until meeting John, had produced only more suffering and endless frustration! But I am still always happy to hang out with John!

Shall we keep this real simple? You say "I exist" but in actual FACT, can you find, in REAL and actual nonconceptual experience, any such existing entity? This is a deeper look into this. Where is any I that exists - ACTUALLY? In simply terms, "you" do NOT exist.

Yet existence appears as all of this - space and apparent content of space - in the timeless Dream Of Oneness.

The final question sometimes appears as "who is asking 'who am I'?" But that question has NO answer. That blankness you describe IS the actuality of infinite being, infinite space, and infinite love.

Who or what is claiming a flip flop, me-and-BE? These are but energy arising as thoughts in Silence and these are never apart from The Silence, are they? This Silence is the Heart, the Substrate, of Consciousness, arising as that life force that makes the body live. Your problem is that you persist in identifying Consciousness as that body-brain-mind machine with it's, thoughts, feelings, experiences, senses, and perceptions. Of course again we come to a paradox: You don't do that! If you were doing it you would assuredly STOP doing it as it brings suffering!

So WHO or WHAT IS doing all this? That is the unanswerable question. Ask YOUR SELF, "What is That which I don't know that I don't know"?

Ponder this from Sri Nisargadatta Maharaj: "What makes you consider yourself a person [with its flip flops etc.]? Your identification with the body. Will this individual personality last? It will remain only so long as long as the identification with the body remains. But once there is a firm conviction that you are not the body, then that individuality is lost. It is the simplest thing, as soon as you have this conviction that you are not the body, then automatically, instantaneously, it is realized that You (the Real One) have always been the manifest totality."

That manifest totality IS your Original nature, already complete and Presencing as the space-like Awareness IN which all that is manifest appears. The point being that Space and Its Content are of Single Essence - Aliveness arising from Nowhere and translated by language as I am, I exist.

Ponder this: You do not exist, and yet, YOU ARE. Nothing/Everything, Wisdom/Love. And your Original Nature is that which is Prior to language. The closest language can come to That is, Being - What I don't know that I don't know. And what You ARE is the Know-ING of THAT.

One without a second, Not Two; pointers to what IS.

That is YOU in Essence.

Form Is Emptiness, Emptiness is Form… like The Man said!

What is endlessly present and aware, right here, right now? Shining silently, yet arising as this activity of Knowing?

Timeless Intelligence, Infinite Energy, One cognizing-emptiness, fully alive, Unborn, and yet, eternally Being?

Here.

Now.

You are That.

What Survives Death?

Q: For many years, my background was in Christianity, but for the last few years I have been steeped in non-duality...reading books, listening to audio downloads, watching videos. I realize that my true nature is awareness and that my old identity just doesn't exist.

C. You say "my". But you do NOT "have" or "own" a True nature. You still seem to think you are a separate entity that owns something called a True Nature. That is a common pitfall in these so called "teachings" and is very misleading.

Q: What has been bothering me lately is, "what is it that survives death?" I realize that my true nature (awareness) survives of course, but is that it? Do we recognize ourselves at all after death? Or do we just fall asleep, have a good dream, and never wake up?

C: Just who is this that would die or be born, survive or not, dream or not? WHO? There is no reality to the assumed identity, EVEN an assumed identity called "I am Awareness". Or "I am everything" or "I am all there is". ALL identities are false, clouds of energy assuming a solidity that just ain't there in FACT...It's all a dream, all a mirage, a lake with no water. The Universe-Appearance is just NO thing LOOKING like everything! Like the mirage lake in the desert LOOKS like water but on closer looking is seen to be absolutely NOTHING.

Q: I sure would appreciate some clarity about this, and I was hoping you could help me out some. I've read all your books, but I just don't find much information that solves my question.

C. Okay, to directly answer the question the way you framed it, in the context in which it is asked:

NO THING SURVIVES DEATH.

NO THING HAS ETERNAL EXISTENCE! ONLY No Thing!

That means, NO THING.

And YOU ARE that ... No Thing.

So, the answer IS pointed to, in the books ... notice what is repeated over and over. Always the mind is challenged to investigate its assumed identity as a "thing" with a solid separate existence. It is the answer the mind gets when the question is asked, "WHO asks the question?" Looking at that right now, what "answerer" is there? There is no answer, no one to answer, no thing at all, just emptiness, spacelike, yet awake and aware as Being-Consciousness-Peace Itself ... and what IS, is The Eternal Nothingness PRIOR to "Consciousness." That is also everything but you will NEVER "know" This ... The Eternal No Thing ... because you ARE This Eternal No Thing appearing as every thing as ALL is ONE Essence of Being Not-A-Something yet Everything. IMPOSSIBLE to grasp. Give that up! Trying to grasp the essence is a loser's game, my friend.

The answer is NOT in or for the mind!

So: There absolutely is NO answer; there IS no "you" that was born and can therefore die. And that IS the answer. All that is born is a false idea of an "I" apart from everything/nothing. That is born and dies. Moment by moment.

As the questioner is always brought back to look, WHO asks this? WHO wants to know? WHO is concerned with this question?

Find that there IS no answer and the question dissolves along with the questioner. And liberation happens, but not for "you". This is liberation from "you" and not for "you".

All there is, is already liberation, already freedom. And so long as there is that veil of assumption, this liberation is forever denied to you. As long as you look for freedom that very freedom that IS remains forever beyond your grasp. But if the frustration with failing to find what you seek becomes potent enough, then there may be a fading of the seeker and a seeing directly for no one that there is nothing to attain, nothing to find, because there never was a "person' who was NOT free. If that happens, then we might call that ... Grace. But no one can make Grace happen!

The bottom line is Nothing Survives Death. And you are THAT ... No THING.

And That is Compassion, and Love, my friend. So BE as you are ... No Thing appearing as Every Dreamlike Thing. And that is all there is for no one to get!

Follow-up:

Q: Wow! Thanks so much. That question was answered so completely and it is very much appreciated. Your answer will take a few readings, but it sure cleared up things nicely. Love and appreciation, and P.S. Thanks for not holding back!

C. You are very welcome, my friend. Stay in touch as and when The One moves that to happen!

This Is It

YOU are BEING. Simply being. Try to NOT BE. Cannot be done. So the simple pointer is, what you are is THAT... all there is is That, what is Real is THAT ... Timeless Being. Just That! This ... BE-ING... is POINTED TO in language with concepts like Impersonal Consciousness; Awareness, Emptiness, No Thing ... or just, Being ... YOU are just THIS ... prior to the mind's language-construct or translation into the thought I Am and I am this or that.

THIS is Impossible to know, impossible to gain, impossible to lose, and if this is "understood", that ... mental understanding ... is NOT This.

"Mental Understanding" is of no value here. That kind of conceptual understanding is, quite simply, the Booby Prize! Yet: The NON-Conceptual Understanding IS that Knowing IS, Being IS. THAT is "Understanding That Belongs To No Owner". No one has That, everyone, and every thing, IS That.

You are NOT an "individual." There are NO "individuals" anywhere except in unreal stories. The idea of a separate person is a fiction, a mind-construction, a house of cards, as the story tries to say, "I'm ME! (Unsuccessfully!) This idea of a "me" is a false claim ... an assertion devoid of authentic evidence ... made by a machine, linguistic machinery ... to it's own separate existence. This ever-changing idea of a person is simply unreal. WHO says "I'm Me?" The mind. To be blunt, it's bullshit. The whole fabricated story of me is pure bullshit; all stories of "individuals" is actually pure fiction. As Shakespeare said, it's a tale told by an idiot, filled with sound and fury, signifying … NOTHING. It's all made up ... by no one!

Where is there any "person"? The "person" is merely a temporary appearance that arises ONLY in "thoughts", subtle words, language. Thoughts come and go. What you ARE NEVER comes and goes anywhere. It is (You Are) fully Here Now and Eternally Free and Clear, the One Eternal Presence.

Look and see that there IS BEING. Being IS, Being is Eternally

No Thing, BEING IS, even before the mentally constructed temporal notions of "here" or "now".

BEING IS. Just THIS as-it-is. There is NO someday when "you" will "get enlightened." It's what you are right now. There is no other than THIS. BEING IS. One Not Two. No Thing appearing as everything. There is nowhere else, there is no one else; there is ONLY BEING. ONLY This. As It IS....

This Is It.

You Are Unborn

Q: It has been said that Consciousness can not be expressed without a mind-body. It's clear that the mind-body is the vehicle with which consciousness expresses itself, but what happens at the apparent death of the mind-body? Is that it - kaput! No more manifestation? However, as Awareness is changeless, then that cannot be true. Awareness must carry on, irrespective of whether the mind-body is alive or dead. What is it that apparently leaves the mind-body at 'death'? This questioning is most likely a distraction, but it keeps popping up. Perhaps it is unanswerable and the answer is the no one really knows. However, I'm sure that you can see the paradox in the question.

C: It IS a distraction, albeit a common one! First off, the FACTS: You are, Being IS. Being is Un-Born, Space-like, empty and meaningless. Timeless, wordless, the a priori Awareness that arises AS consciousness arises AS the knowingness, "I AM", the sense of Presence that is always here PRIOR to the "languaging" or the words "I am". I AM prior to I am, so to say. Your true nature is formless; this body-mind with its sense "I am" is the coat that formlessness wears; like the clothes of the naked emperor. The emperor never was clothed; it was a believed illusion dispelled by the innocence of looking without conceptualizing, the child in that metaphor of "The emperor's new clothes".

Being IS. You are That and Nothing else. That's a FACT. ALL else is mind stuff, speculation, wanting an answer to know something that will make the mind feel secure for a time. The question I would suggest you ask yourself, is "WHO is asking this question, and why?" Why do you want an answer? What will an answer provide for you that you do not already have? What is fully present and clear right now, IN which consciousness itself, and then the arising question, both appear? Questions are arising thoughts. To fixate on a question requires that you assume there is "someone" in there asking; a questioner. But where IS the questioner? Who is asking that question and of whom?

Nothing was "born" and nothing "leaves the body at death". What dies is only the notion, the belief, "I AM". That Consciousness needs fuel, like a candle wick needs the fuel of the wax to burn. The food body is the fuel for consciousness. Awareness is UNBORN... you ARE Awareness, unaware OF "things" yet always "ON", forever Self-Knowing, Eternal Self, Being without consciousness ... and That is what You are, in truth. "Know the Truth of what you are and Know that You are freedom. Life, Light". Whatever the label, you are That which the label points at.

You are Unborn. Full Stop. All that was born is the "sense-I-Am". That "you" dies every night in sleep. You don't ask, "where did 'I' go in sleep", do you? So that is what dying is like to consciousness, but "birth and death" are happenings in Life Itself, AKA YOU, What You Are. Changeless forever.

Forever means forever!

What Is "Born" That Could "Die"?

Q: You and I are both past 60 and retired. That means the final chapter, (in each of our stories), is relentlessly approaching. Your book...."From I Am to I Am, With Love", has got me thinking. Granted, the thinking me is not really me. I am awareness. Yet how do you regard your inevitable (physical) death? Nothing to it? No self, no worries, no problem?

These thoughts were perhaps triggered by the recent death of Ramesh Balsekar. If thoughts are really nothing, would you mind sharing your thoughts on this inevitability? With warm appreciation for your book, and continued Facebook presence...

C. You are very welcome; glad this sharing is "resonating!"

You have asked a good question! Here is how it is here: Every night when this "charlie-thing" goes to bed, it "dies" ... that is the sense "I Am" is not there; Consciousness is in abeyance. What is born in the morning is only the "I Am". That is Consciousness, as you know.

Now it gets tricky. If "I Am" is appearing as Consciousness, it is clear that this "I Am" IS a thing appearing TO Awareness; Awareness is the Eternal Being, PRIOR to, Permeating, and "allowing" for the happening of ... Consciousness. As a language distinction, notional only, Awareness is NOT Consciousness, and I AM (You ARE, There is ONLY) Awareness, No Thing, never born. And of course there cannot be TWO "No Things". This is the true meaning of "I AM THAT" (So-Ham"), or THAT THOU ART (Tat Tvam Asi). There is ONLY That....

So: To answer the question in the context you asked it, my direct, actual experience is that there is NO concern regarding physical death. I have pondered this. And the way it is here, or in street language what it's like for "me", is this:

Crystal clear is the fact ... FACT ... that this "I, I Am," was never born! It APPEARS that a thing is born every morning and dies every night (or sometimes in the afternoon if a nap happens :-)) ... but WHO is born that could die? WHO!??

Plainly said, I AM THAT BY which "I Am" is known. The Knowing Light doesn't "know itself". Our beloved Ramesh was never born so how could he die? That said, some of the human energy-patterns "left behind in the earth dream" will likely experience moments of sadness or a sense of loss. I did. Along with a sense of real joy that Ramesh no longer has to fuss with an aging body so to speak! But none of that is the case for Ramesh! If you die today, will you care?? Who would be there? Not "you".

So in the final analysis, the whole issue is moot, for the Die-ee"!

Don't know if this will answer it for you fully, but as always, a final point might well be to look, "Who asks the question?" and "Who wants to know?" which if there are traces of assumed identity lingering can erase the trace in this Instant-Before-Time....

So in street words, I could give a bleep if this charlie-thing dies now. Any day is a good day to die! I knew Ramesh well enough to know he would have said something like this too. The "knower-of-Reality" doesn't fear death at all, for him it is just the final return to Home. I love how the sages talk about the "event" ... they named it "Maha-Samadhi" which I translate as "The Great Peace". And the point so to say of Nonduality is, as the Zen sage Bankei puts it, to "Die before you die". That death of the false assumption of being a separate self IS the "Peace that passeth understanding".

In truth, "you" don't have a "physical self". The appearance of a body only implies a separate self. But investigation proves to "the mind" once and for good that no such self exists! So the collection of cells formed of energy changes form. The Self that you are will forever remain unchanging, free and clear of any identity as a body. Look into that assumption "my physical self". The body is not "yours". That idea of "mine", of being an owner, is right at the heart of ignorance of Self and the assumption that separateness, twoness, is the reality. It is NOT.

Knowing the Self as what we are removes all traces of concern for whether a machine (bodymind) stops running. He knows that the machine is temporal, a momentary appearance, where What Is, cannot die. The Electricity that runs a toaster and a fridge doesn't die when the toaster or fridge stops working. In the same way the Energy (Shakti) that powers a heart beating doesn't die when the heart stops.

In this Understanding (which belongs to no one!) lies perfect peace. And this IS deeply understood by everyone; it's just gotten apparently obscured by the false sense of self (mind, or ego) that appears IN The Self (and as the manifest ASPECT of Self).

You Are Unborn. That is the bottom line.

You, like me, are that One No Thing appearing as some things, and every thing. That's it.

Bottom line: YES, no worries, no concern, no problem!

Wherever You Go. HERE, You ARE

Wherever you go you are ... Here. Whatever the 'timepiece' indicates, it is ... Now. Here and Now. Now and Here. (NoWHere). What's wrong with Now? What's missing in Here? This Here-Now is Presence, Awareness, Emptiness ... Loving what IS.

What IS, Is. And That's THAT. ..... The pointer comes, "I Am That; Thou Art That, there is ONLY That". What IS That? THAT IS. Just IS. And so ... Here and Now: That's THAT.

That's What?

Awareness, Content, Everything.

EVERY NO THING .... Just That.

What Is Beyond Knowing?

It is often said "being is knowing". In fact that is what my blog is called (got to call it something, I suppose). But the more potent expression might be a question: "What is beyond knowing"?

ANY answer is impotent and irrelevant... what is that which IS, beyond seeing, knowing, even beyond being?

No answer.

Open question, Open Secret ...

What Am I?

Q: Okay, I have asked who am I? What am I?, like Ramana Maharshi's and Nisargadatta Maharaj's books say I need to do. You also mention that kind of investigation in your books. There doesn't seem to be any answer. All I get is an empty silence. So now my question is, WHAT AM I really and truly and how come I can't find an answer?

C: Good question, First off, the end of seeking consists in not knowing any answer. So NO answer is THE answer. It is in the failure to grasp any answer that the natural Seeing is unconcealed.

Secondly: The concept for what is seen directly is, what you are is the Space IN which both the question and the assumed question-ER appear and disappear. That Space ... Being-seeing-Knowing-ness ... never changes ever. You are not the concept space. You are the ACTUAL Space. THAT is the essence and formless energy that appears as all that is, THAT is both empty and filled with joy and aliveness, love and vitality. In a Zen way of pointing That is both everything and nothing. Full stop.

To paraphrase 'Sailor' Bob Adamson, the questioner is the question. They cancel each other out. What remains? Space, this bare naked presence-awareness. No Thing. You are That, I Am That, Nothing is That, and Everything is That.

Precisely What Is "The I"?

We all say "I" when referring to the organism in our most immediate view, a thing with a name and a form. That we "think of" as "my" form with "my" name (erroneously!)

But what actually IS this "I"? The ancient sages had a bit to say about this: They pointed out that the only "I" is pure being. They called it "Purno 'ham Vimarsha"; the Pure I Consciousness.

What do YOU mean by "I"? What is the word "I" referring to? Is there a separate I there and a separate I here? How could there be "multiple" "I"s? Is it your conviction that the "I" you are and the "I" your next door neighbor, or your spouse, or your mother is, are all "different" "I"s?

There is but One I. That Universal I is nothing ... No Thing, Non-Conceptualizable, AKA Naked Being, or Pure Open Awareness. Of course, This Real I cannot be described, so take these words for what they are: POINTERS ONLY to the Timeless Reality that You really are.

Looking from another angle, this "I" word is obviously a concept. Is any concept the actuality represented by that concept? Take the word "fire". You can shout the word as loud as you like but that word will never burn anything! Isn't that obvious? You are not stupid; you know that "fire" doesn't burn a thing or light a flame to cook your food. There is another example: can you eat the word "food"? Of course not.

If this seems over-simplified and pedantic, stay with me: have another look at the word "I".

You may say, I am reading this. But what does this mean? I might say "I am writing this"; who or what IS that I that "I say" to point to an organism apparently acting, and "you also say" or use to point to an organism apparently acting? Is that a true representation? Are you a thing? Are you the one letter word "I"? No. So while I say "I am writing here", and you say "I am reading here", isn't there the clear Present Knowing that Awareness is writing to Awareness!? With no "I-the-doer?" So to speak... Is it not clear when investigating in this way, that The

One I is all there is and just apparently doing all of this that appears? Who assumes otherwise? Only a phantom self that has no basis in Reality. A passing thought-form, no more real than a ghost.

Have a closer look: is that "I" thought always there? And is something that is not always here and/or always there going to really fit an intelligent definition of what is REAL? When the "I" is taken to refer to a thing separate from the Whole, suffering ensues. When the "I" is seen to refer to Absolutely Nothing, it becomes merely a tool for communication in the relative appearance. No problem, as long as the I is not taken on board as "me" vs. "not me".

The I word, when seen as a pointer, makes it obvious that "I" points only to Awareness, or Beingness. This Being-That-You-Are is NOT a concept, NOT a thing that is sometimes present and sometimes absent.

So what IS the Eternal I-Beingness that the word "I" points to?

If the I is not TWO, then when you say "I" and I say "I", we are both pointing to what is Eternal, The One Always-So Naked Nonconceptual Awareness.

And is there any problem with Naked Awareness? NO.

You Are That.

My Problem Is Fear

Q: My problem is fear. Fear to be nothing. Fear to be everything. When the identities slip there is freedom - then something grasps, clings; to the familiar, learned, ephemeral illusion of 'me-with-a-name'. Then comes the pain, which seems so real. The universe does not begin where the skin stops - there is no me and then the universe. But the identity is sooooooo seductive Charlie! To quote Trent Reznor (popular pop artists) - "... the pain, the only thing that's real." Or seems to be real.

C: Pain is part of an organism's natural functioning and signals an area of the bodymind that needs attention, medical care. Suffering is an entirely different matter. In "From I Am to I Am, With Love" I make a distinction between these two as follows in "Suffering is Optional"...

Suffering Is Optional.

Suffering and pain are distinct.

How?

Basically, pain is a signal that something is not working in the organism. Dogs have pain. Humans have pain. But the dog does not suffer — because the dog does not have a sense of being a separate psychological entity that takes ownership of the pain—and as the owner, that entity adds the secondary idea that the pain "should not be."

The sage Nisargadatta Maharaj pointed to this perfectly. Late in his life his body was wracked with pain from cancer. One time a visitor asked him as he saw him wincing, "Maharaj, are you in great pain?" The sage replied, "There IS great pain."

This is quite illuminating when looked into. "There IS great pain" acknowledges a condition of the body but makes no claim to owning that pain. In Presence Awareness, anything can arise. But it is NOT "taken on board." When Charlie's back or arthritis hurts it is not MY pain. There is no suffering unless there's the FALSE me-mine split in the thought-story.

All that arises is simply what IS... and is not a personal matter. Once it is seen that what we ARE is Presence Awareness and what we are NOT is "an individual," the game is over; you can no longer believe that pain is personal — any more than you can believe the earth is flat.

It may take some deep looking for this to be seen... especially if there is severe pain. For example, being wracked by spasms of coughing may seem to take the attention so completely to the body that the awareness appears to have been "forgotten." But in actual fact is the awareness ever really missing? No. It cannot be.

Possibly what is needed in these instances is to look, as soon as possible, into what it is that is in pain or suffering about there being a wracking cough. We say or think, "I am coughing. I am in pain." We add on to the awareness "I Am" and say I am in pain. Making a sharp distinction between this "I Am" awareness and that which has pain... the body-mind organism... does the trick. When the sword of razor sharp discrimination is brought to bear on this business of the thought story "I am in pain," then it is seen... effortlessly... that FIRST is I. I is just Awareness. Oneness. I-I, as the sage Ramana Maharshi referred to it. Then next comes I AM... Awareness, arising as Consciousness. Pure knowingness, no subject-object split; just the knowing Existence Is and I Am That.

THEN comes the mischief made of the thought machinery... the mind. The MIND says I am this BODY, and that is taken on board by the I Am as a belief in something real called "my body."

That's the trigger for suffering, as the mind adds on, "I am in pain, I don't like that, I want that to change, why is this happening to me"? Poor me! Etc."

Notice that all this is pinned to a core belief in the identification with the body! And yet, where is the body except in a thought story appearing presently?

Making the distinction between the pure I Am, Awareness-Presence, and the thoughts that arise IN that Awareness, makes all the difference in seeing that while there may well be pain for one who has seen his or her True Nature, there is NO suffering, because suffering is only possible for the fictional person. Once that "person" has been seen to be nothing more than thoughts, based on a belief in a separate "me" thing identified as a body with a name, etc., the game is over.

The End of Suffering

When you find out that the earth is round you no longer buy into the story that you dare not sail out too far or you'll fall off... once you know beyond doubt that the phantom is a ghost and is not real, the energy of belief no longer goes into that phantom "me" and its stories. Therein lies authentic freedom from all psychological suffering

The end of suffering is simple: Start with the only FACT you know: I AM. Just That! Then: Investigate who sees, who thinks, who you are, and see the false nature of the "one who suffers." Then remain as you are... Presence Awareness, just that. Simple and natural. Home.

"Pain is physical, suffering is mental. Beyond the mind there is no suffering. Pain is essential for the survival of the body, but none compels you to suffer. Suffering is due entirely to clinging or resisting; it is a sign of our unwillingness to move on, to flow with life. As a sane life is free of pain, so is a saintly life free from suffering. A saint does not want things to be different from what they are; he knows that, considering all factors, they are unavoidable. He is friendly with the in-evitable and, therefore, does not suffer. Pain he may know, but it does not shatter him. If he can, he does the needful to restore the lost balance, or he lets things take their course." — Sri Nisargadatta Maharaj

Ponder the above carefully!

Q: There was abuse in childhood - the survival instinct is sharply honed, and very industrious. When all encumbrances drop - there is love and peace and joy. What could be the problem regarding my true self as THAT? Cynicism? What is this fear to be nothing?

C: The answer is in the question. It is the fear to be nothing. The mind has had identities for so long as this or that thing, starting with "I am I" and "this "I" is me, my body, my thoughts, my perceptions, my feelings; my self is "me" ... that when the assumption that "I am separate and there is something wrong with me" gets challenged that core of false identity can try to avoid being "outed" as the ghost that is really is. All suffering is merely mental and based on memory, arising as "I-thoughts" in awareness, presently. Presently arising thoughts are not a problem unless there is a fixation on them as being a "me" or "about a me". The subtle assumption "I am a separate me with all these issues and problems" is the culprit.

That sense of life as a "me" is ONLY an unchallenged assumption. That is why we spend a lot of time inviting the seeker to mount a sincere and earnest challenge to that core assumption. An assumption is NOT true. It is ONLY an assumed reality but on looking for actual evidence of its existence, no such authentic evidence can ever be found! Shine the Light of Naked Awareness on that assumption! All issues, problems and suffering are based only of the acceptance of a false assumption as true. But when you seek evidence for the existence of this sufferer, the "me", ALL you find is empty space. You ARE that empty space, No Thing. What kicks back in and "gets scared" IS false; make no mistake about this. Root that assumption out at the very core. The pure Light of Naked Awareness is your natural state and all else is the fruits and flowers of ignorance arising from that one unchallenged assumption. So look head on at that sense of "me" and find evidence for its reality. You will never find proof of its actual substance because it has none.

All you find in staring head on at the mind is self-reinforcing thoughts... "Who am I"? I am ME". But where is the "me" located? It is not real, any more than a ghost is real. It is childish to keep believing in such things as ghosts or Santa Claus or bogeymen in the closet. The key is in understanding what is actually real; the assumption "there IS a Santa Claus" is NO different than the assumption "there is a 'me'". So dig in, my friend. Dig in!

"Start with the solid fact of your being and have a good look at that. That sense of being is, in truth, all this is about. Therefore, the beginning is also the end." ~ *John Wheeler*

Words Are Only Pointers

And, the map is NOT the territory; the signpost is not the town.

Q: I'm reading I AM THAT at the moment. There are two statements made by Nisargadatta in this book that seem to contradict each other, and on a subject which is at the heart of this non-duality stuff: Recently what has taken place often with "me" is that I just am still, looking at whatever is. That was until I came across the second of the two statements I quote here from the book. As they say, "WTF!?" (what the bleep.)

Could you fill me in on what I'm missing here please, I'd be very grateful...

Questioner: To know perfectly I need a perfect mind. Nisargadatta: A quiet mind is all you need.

And in another place:

Nisargadatta: If you want peace you must strive for it. You will not get peace just by keeping quiet.

C: Certainly, and it's a good question. As I see this apparent "dilemma" (your WTF? Comment): Essentially it is that Maharaj was talking to two different people with different mental confusions. There is a great danger in trying to parse out "correct concepts". NO concept is right; they are all only pointers. So quite often two apparently contradictory points can come out!

You say what has been happening for you is being just still, looking at what is. That is a temporary state, as you are finding out. Some influence arises and bang! You are no longer "just still". What does this show you? Can you see that "stillness" is not all it's cracked up to be when it is "my" stillness? Happening to "me"?

The assumed-as-real-me is the core issue. What exactly IS this me? Where is it? What is it made of? Can you find a real, separate me? Or when you look at what is actually there, what do you find? Nothing! Space-like awareness.

What you are is that naked awareness and that is what registers the stillness and the movement out of stillness. If there is a sense of witnessing, that witnessing is also a passing state, and all passing states pass! What is that which does not pass away?

What Is THAT which is ALWAYS Present and aware? Always "on", always simply present yet not present as a thing? Presence is No Thing. Any thing has a beginning and an end. Simple naked presence-awareness does not begin nor does it end (because it is NOT an "it" actually). That, not-a-thing beingness, is forever unaltered, unmodified, and forever free of taint or change. You are THAT. Do assume the existence of a separate person with some attributes like stillness or agitation? Or is that JUST an assumption? Is it true that you are a changing thing? Are you the body? Are you IN the body? Or are all those just ideas, thoughts, language ... appearing IN your unchanging true nature of naked awareness?

Find that separate me and show it to me. Can you? Looking in this way, can you actually find anything substantial and solid? Or do you just see and feel passing thoughts and feelings that have no reality apart from the validity you yourself give them by self-reinforcing words? "I am me. I know I am me because I think and believe I am me". It is, for most of us, a long standing habit to assume ... ASSUME ... that what we think is who we are. But is it? "I am me!" Is that assertion TRUE? Where is your evidence? Only in the mental reaffirming of that statement, and nowhere else. So the delusion is purely mental. It's just words! And words come and go. The identity you take your self to be, whether that is a really big serene identity such as "I am stillness" or "I am naked awareness", or "I am a little insecure me", are only conceptual word-structures. LANGUAGE.

And, there is NO identity in deep sleep, where Awareness is fully present and "living" the body but not conscious of being; without that waking sense of "I am", yet fully and forever alive and real.

That awareness-unaware-of-itself IS the eternal "knower" of any and all relative states, which are appearances that arise and subside IN that.

You are that changeless awareness. Challenge that assumption that you are some thing that can change. You are not. Uncovering the false self center is done by investigation, looking directly within the silent words of the mind, the subtle mental movement, or background of an assumed premise of separation, to locate the source, the nexus. That core or nexus is ONLY an assumption. We assume there is a core point called me and then believe that is who we are; and that core assumption is the root of confusion and suffering. Root it out through investigation. Where is that core "me" sense"? Go on the hunt for it. Get really into the investigation, like a scientist delving into the nature of what appears real, until it's clear that what you are is not a separate entity with any problems whatsoever.

All words, as I said, are only pointers; signposts if you like, indicating something completely overlooked, and unseen until the signpost shows you where to look.

Take the words of Sri Nisargadatta for what they are … pointers, showing not what you will find, but where to look. For example, he said ""Stay with the I AM". He clarified: Not the concept of thought "I am", but rather your simple sense of presence, of your very undeniable BEING; that knowing beingness that is translated in concepts as I am. Knowing that NO concept is the real, but only a description or representation, seek to find the real NON-conceptual I AM ness and stay with that. Then he added "Give up all questions except one: 'Who am I'?" Look deeply into the sense of presence, the knowing of your own inescapable Beingness. Find out where this I thought-sense originates. What it is made of. Find out if that thought is really who you are. It is not. But get the evidence for yourself. Shine the light of awareness-presence on the assumption and let that light reveal the truth of what you are.

Get down to the bottom of this and know thy Self.

End Game

Q: I have a question: I have had now a few glimpses and the thought comes into say that "that is it and this is not it"....

C: Thoughts are completely irrelevant. Any thought can arise. Does the thought touch what You ARE? That Naked Awareness? This denuded beingness which is the constant background and always fully present at all "times" is YOU, your True Nature. No thought can get within a million miles of that because THAT is what IS, always JUST SO. That never is altered or affected in any way by a thought or other appearance, in the same way the cinema screen is untouched by the play of images and sounds apparently coming from it but in fact those appearances cannot BE unless the screen is there to register them. In exactly the same way this Present Aware Beingness registers all that appears while remaining utterly untouched by whatever seems to appear. Get that point firm first!

Q: Things like not being able to find myself in a room, seeing this ME appearing in what I am, feeling disorientated in a room with other people and not knowing which one of these people AM I supposed to be, and then having to remind myself.. I am this one with the glasses, hearing sounds without a me there to hear those sounds, i.e. that there is just a sound, the sensation of feeling like a bazillion tiny pieces and that they implode back to being a thought. Like the universe imploding back on to a thought of ME, and most recently the sensation of the world being a movie screen that is just happening.

C: Okay now that is quite a story! But is that story YOU? No. You are That which COGNIZES that story and all that you describe is just like a thunderstorm happening while the sky, the space, forever remains empty, serene and untouched. The question as always is WHO is this that feels disoriented, believes he is the one with glasses, feels like being in tiny pieces etc? WHO? Take it back to the core: Who AM I that thinks, sees, feels, knows, or doesn't know, anything at all? Who are YOU? Are YOU an object appearing, coming and going? Or NOT? The essence of this is to fully dismantle that "furball" of false conceptions of who you are; you are NOT anything that thoughts can grasp, own or know. Take it apart thread by thread. NOT this NOT this. You must continue to be earnest, and willing to REJECT ANY identifying thought. While there is clearly some good Seeing happening, this cul-de-sac of identity must be fully deconstructed for the peace that you are to be completely clear (even though it is already utterly free and clear yet the believed-identity SEEMS to obstruct it so that has to be dismantled.)

Ponder this bit of pointing which I wrote to another "seeker":

Q: But who is to expose or dismantle it?

C: That "you that still says I, I am this person, I still suffer. That "you" that is only a passing idea, energy-sound in Awareness, yet that idea is being taken to be real. To be "you!" Challenge that! Don't just buy into some "nondual platitude" like "there is no one so who will look"? That is a ploy the ego-ideation uses to avoid its own being outed as the fake it really is. The emperor doesn't want to be found out to have no clothes. YOU are Naked Awareness. Any idea to the contrary needs to be investigated and dismantled. The search began in the mind so the challenge to our cherished assumption of "I am I, Me" MUST be taken on IN that very mind. This is a paradox to the mind that wants the security of an answer. The "Answer" "there is no one" will still leave you suffering, as you are admitting when you are being honest about your actual experience. In my experience the structure of conceptualizing consists of: A): Interpretations of what is, including judgments and evaluations of what "should be different" or "could be better" that what simply IS; B): The fixation that "what is appearing is a real happening and it's all happening to ME; and C): The core assumption that I AM the THOUGHT-BELIEF I, Me, My Self in a World Out There which I am separate from;, and D): There IS a location for ME and there is also TIME, a past and future, which constrains ME.

Q: So these mysterious glimpses or experiences bring about the thought that this here now is not it and those experiences are it. Even if they are incredibly ordinary these are still a fundamentally and totally different perspective of this life. That cannot be denied; and why is this not it is because it feels like it is surrounded by thought.

Deconstruct that! ALL experiences are passing appearances while your True Self NEVER moves, NEVER changes, it is THAT Which Always IS, as JD Hazlewood puts it.

Q: I am earnest... Nothing else is really happening in my life apart from this. And not a moment goes by where I am not checking myself.

C: Good. But go easy on yourself. Make it a curiosity to discover the source of suffering, rather than making this a "demand" or some overly aggressive challenge. Be a bit gentle yet firmly interested, curious to uncover what is at the core of it all. In other words, give yourself some love and compassion here, my friend.

Q: These experiences are a bit of a blocker at the moment, as the feeling or thought is...that or those experiences are where I need to get to.

C: That is exactly correct in the way you state it, and YET, these "blocks" are also the great opportunity to go deeper into True Understanding ... to "Stand Under" what appears to be blockages and see that it's all imagination, based only on the taking your self to be a CONCEPT. YOU were NEVER a concept; YOU Are Unborn Being, free and clear, and seeing this takes you out of the conceptualizing game (in which there is no joy, as you are aware!)

Stay with it. Asking Who Am I that still takes on board the odious idea of a me that is flawed and incomplete. Who Am I? That thought reveals NO answer; it unconceals the Space, the Awareness, that You ARE. Stay with THAT and let THAT show you the depths of Its emptiness and the richness of Its fullness.

Keep on. You are at the end game. Don't quit now! I Love You.

The Root Cause Of Suffering

The cause of suffering is fixation on a concept:

A friend writes, Even though the root cause is seen as illusionary, the suffering does remain (in fact because it is exposed now, it can be even more intense).

C: My friend: If any suffering remains, then that root has NOT been fully exposed and dismantled! Where IS the "I" that makes THIS claim? Who says that suffering has been exposed? This claim is made by an ego that resists being REALLY seen and dismantled! Keep looking, dig down and locate the real Source of the I thought; that one thought "I" is the fixative and the fixation, the "glue" is that energy of belief going into a false self center that on earnest and committed investigation simply cannot be found! Root out that cause and the effects die on the vine of True Seeing. Start from the one FACT you are certain of: I AM. Look for the SOURCE of this I AM-NESS that you know is so. No one can tell you, you are not. That sense of presence, of Existingness, is all you know by direct knowing rather than conceptualizing. Suffering can only consist and persist in conceptualizing self as a separate suffering thing ... "poor me", "woe is me", etc.

What we point out is that the root cause must be ELIMINATED. Seeing the mechanism is a first step, for sure. But to challenge the mind's assertions of belief until that cause is DISMANTLED is what is said to be the "means"...

Get real with this. Suffering is optional!

It's Already Fully Shining, Right Here Right Now

Q: Nisargadatta repeatedly exhorted listeners to watch the sense 'I Am', and said that it took him three years of doing this before he finally realized his true nature. On the other hand, he also maintained that it takes absolutely no effort to realise Who You Really Are.

C: You could go mad trying to resolve the apparent contradictions ... just know that ALL concepts are ONLY pointers and NOT some "truth".

Q: [A British teacher] has repeatedly suggested that any practice or any effort to become self-realized is dualistic and re-enforces the sense of separation because it implies that there is somebody who can do something to attain liberation. He says that there is already only ever awakeness. What is your take on all this?

C: Sure, there IS only ever "awakeness" or "wholeness". Being-Awareness IS all there is. All is ONE. So in a way that is true. BUT ... if there is still suffering, then isn't it obvious that there IS still the assumption of a person seeking operating in the mind? If there is the assumption there IS a "person", a suffering "me", no amount of "opposition by assertion" or some dogmatic "affirmation" will change that. ONLY investigation into the mechanics of the root cause of our human suffering will work to disengage the fixation on a phantom (yet ignorantly assumed real) "me" to whom "stuff happens" ... as so many authentic sages such as Sri Nisargadatta, Ramana Maharshi and current ones like Bob Adamson and John Wheeler have pointed out.

Q: I find that trying to be aware of the present moment does take effort. I understand that even when I am deeply attending to the past or the future and to thinking that I am still only presence-awareness, but this understanding does not seem enough to eliminate suffering from my experience.

C: But does it take any "effort" to BE? No. YOU ARE. Try to NOT BE. It's inescapable. Being IS and That Thou Art.

Now: Do you know the cause of suffering? You say I this and I that. But if there is "only awakeness" and no "person", no "I", then exactly WHO is this asserted I that is claiming a presence that is obviously a belief in being an individual apart from wholeness? You can't have it both ways!

Q: There seems to be a difference between understanding that all there is, is pure awareness manifesting as an apparently real dream and being in a state in which one abides as that awareness, and that some sort of effort to bring about that state is necessary (for example, spending three years watching the sense 'I Am').

C: But you never can NOT abide as Awareness despite what the mind claims. Awareness is ALWAYS SO. Now it also sounds like you may have adopted some "there is no one so who would investigate" dogmatic belief about this stuff. Let's get real. Are you suffering? You are indicating that you are. Questioning, looking for answers or reasoning this all out, IS suffering! So, are you seeking some "special state" that you will get for the I identity? The "me"? It seems so, right? So let's address that.

Q: Nisargadatta said that 'understanding is all', but I can understand it intellectually and yet I still experience suffering. I still get stressed out when I have too much to do and not enough time to do it in. I still have concerns about survival. I still have moments when I just do not feel like I can accept something that is painful or feels bad.

C: Good, now it's getting down to what matters to YOU. Right here just NOTICE the constant affirming of the existence of an "I". That thought is the root. The energy of belief goes into that "I thought" and that gets taken to be who you are. But you are NOT a thought; all thoughts, which are only concepts, including that "I" concept, come and go while the Present Awakeness or Awareness that is REAL and always "on" NEVER comes and goes, NEVER changes. That "always-so-ness" of Being, Aware Presence, is the ever-open and empty background, the necessary condition for any thought to appear. You are THAT and ONLY THAT is Eternal, Real... So: The issue here is an assumption that you ARE the I thought, and until that is investigated and found to be a mirage, a phantom, the suffering goes on and on. So WHO is this I? Is it REAL? Only that which cannot and does not change can be the Reality, the natural, the eternal. Seeing yourself as a thought, you suffer. YOU are NO concept, NO word can define you. Pointers like Being, Awareness, I Am-ness, are all ONLY pointing to That which is always fully present and aware regardless of what appears in or on that open space-like Is-ness. Remember, what You are is NOT a concept, NOT a word, NOT a thing that language can ever grasp or describe. The closest might be, "You Are No Thing", as Bob Adamson sometimes points out your True Self. It is That which just ... IS.

Q: Although I understand intellectually that there is no 'me' and that there can be no 'me', there is nevertheless a sense that there is a 'me'. If I try to get rid of the sense of 'me', then there is an apparent 'me' trying to get rid of itself, thus re-enforcing itself (that British teacher all over again). If I keep coming back to the understanding that there is no 'me', there still seems to be a 'me' anyway. What to do?

C: Investigate! What is needed is to:

A) realize that suffering has a cause,

B) remove the cause and the effects cannot stand, and,

C) understand the actual mechanics of suffering.

For some just asking the mind, who says this? Who am I? Is enough to disengage the false connection between what is said or seen or thought about, and the sense of "this is happening to ME". More often a little guidance is needed, from one whose understanding is clear, as to what the mechanics of this suffering really are. For me, John Wheeler's guidance was indispensable. So if you are open to it, we might have a talk on Skype or by phone to get down to the root of this.

ALL suffering is, is self-centered thinking, coming out from the deeply held belief-assumption that "I AM this individual, this self I call 'me'." Until that is dismantled at the core, suffering goes on, despite all the protestations the mind mounts against that dismantling. One clever ploy the mind uses to avoid the phantom "me" being seen and ousted is this notion "there is no one so who would look and dismantle." That is a mental justification that leads most often to profound resignation, a kind of "personal hopelessness", and deep despair. Been there done that. It's no fun. But the good news is, there IS a proven means to end suffering!

Nisargadatta showed that to Bob. Bob showed that to John Wheeler. John showed that to me. Now it's your turn … IF you are open.

To know the reality of what you are, Being, only That, empty yet full, is the true gift of imbibing these pointers. The beauty in this is, you ARE and you already KNOW that. No one can ever tell you "you are not being". Nor can you honestly tell yourself that. The I AM is the ONLY certainty; it's your own absolute, incontrovertible, intimate knowing, that being IS. That is REAL for you, right? That's IT, my friend. The whole thing is that Being IS and You Are THAT. To know thyself as That, Naked Being, and to rediscover what you are NOT, and that nothing that happens or appears is the real You, is the profound gift and legacy of the great sages.

So why not get onto the REAL understanding, which is beyond "intellect" or "reason", and come back Home to what you truly are?

It's already here now. Just take it! It's YOURS.

No Concept Can Define Your Natural Beingness

Q: There still seems to exist a duality in "me". Even though that duality can't be real. On the one hand, the person is not there and instead there is nothing, a vast vacuum or space or eternal sea where no ripple can be created. Focusing on that is blissful.

C: Well perhaps but that is a pendulum swing and the other side of it is suffering! Blissful states are temporary. All states are temporary and NOT what we are pointing to as your True Self!

Q: I like that expression, "Eternal Sea where no ripple can be created".

C: That's really not all that clear. The ripples are the same essence of water as the sea: This is NOT TWO. In the same way as that sea, your essence of pure Awareness and all the seemingly separate appearances are ALL that same essence. Not Two.

Q: And on the other hand it is not being understood or seen how this space, nothingness or whatever is also everything. "Form is emptiness and emptiness is form". That doesn't quite compute here for some reason. The nothingness is more like, well, just simply nothing, and not even nothing, because "nothing" is just a word. How the everything is the same as that, or one with it, is not seen.

C: Can there be two no things? Oneness IS No Thing NOT Two... Also, "everything" is also just a word, a concept. NO concept can ever capture or define what you are! The No Thing is NOT a thing that the mind can grasp or own; Awareness, No Thing, is NOT personal and NOT an object with properties. It appears that there is still a subtle fixation on being "someone" who is somehow defective because "it is not being understood". Do you need to understand this to BE? Awareness is absolutely no thing and that means NO thing. Yet "IT", that No Thing, is fully infused with Freedom and Aliveness; we call that Aliveness Simply Being-Knowing! Life Being Life. Your Real Self. All just pointers, LOOK where the words point TO. Whatever we call THAT, it IS and THAT is beyond doubt. Right? You IS.

Full Stop!

Please start out from the one FACT you cannot escape or deny: You ARE. Being IS! Irrefutable. Or Awareness IS. That true nature is never not here and never touched by any concept or object. But to make "no thing" into an object will also lead to making "everything" into ANOTHER separate object. This will keep the tacitly assumed self-center (the pre-verbal "I AM the me" assumption) in place and keep the mind spinning in this confusion.

But the idea of being someone is ONLY a passing fancy and a learned notion adopted by a two-year-old's brain and imbedded and it kind of has turned solid. But it is NOT actually solid when looked directly into.

This is why investigation must happen to root out the false assumption that "there IS a 'me' and that 'me' IS real". It's a belief and NOT what actually IS. It takes discrimination and looking, rather than stopping at some assertion like "I am no thing" because that statement will just become another definition pasted onto your true indefinable nature.

Q: But is there really a need for that understanding? I mean, who is trying to understand it?

C: What is needed is the understanding of A) what you ARE and B) the mechanics of suffering and assumed separation. That is essential. That's what is shared here.

Q: And I notice how I put that in the terms of "on the one hand...and on the other hand", like there are two separate things when in fact there is not. But still that understanding is not being felt and understood here... or is that just the fake person sneaking up from the shadows like a zombie creating a kind of separation?

C: No explanation will satisfy because what wants an explanation is a false self that has no more real existence than Santa Claus. And who is this "I" that says "I notice?" "I put..." etc? Where is it?

What is that I-assumption, that self-center, actually made of?

Presently arising thoughts, appearing in the empty space of your true nature of Awareness.

The crucial point is that the culprit is that an intrinsically meaningless I-thought is being given an "assumed reality". It is a kind of spiritual immaturity; like still believing in Santa Claus who, once the child is a few years older, is seen to be a totally false assumption. This is no different! See through this by looking in at the mind's chatter from your natural timeless state of aware presence. That is never missing and there is never anything wrong in and as That. Abide as That and LOOK...

Shine the natural light of that naked "I AM" Awareness on the false belief. It's like sneaking downstairs and seeing that there is no Santa Claus; seeing daddy putting the presents out under the tree, and mommy drinking the milk you left out, and eating the cookies... where in the past you took the presents and the remaining crumbs and empty milk glass as your "proof" of the existence of Santa.

Also, take NO identification on board, EVEN an identity called "I am no thing" OR "I am everything."

ALL identities are false. Even to assert I am Wholeness is FALSE. What You ARE is just plain everyday Awareness and there is NOTHING "wrong" with THAT.

Looking into this business of "a duality in 'me'", WHO assumes there is a defective "me" that lacks some understanding? Ask this until the falseness of that assumption is seen clearly: What IS this "I" or "me" that "wants to understand and/or experience itself as being everything?" Where is that thing? IS that a thing, with a beginning, middle and end?

Find out; see for yourself, that the ignorance-assumption of separateness, of a "me", is merely a thought-assumption construct made of air. What is that "thing" that wants more than naked awareness?

That true self is freedom itself. WHO wants more than freedom?

Bottom line is YOU are NOT a thing and yet Awareness ...

Being-Aliveness … your True Nature … IS. Always. Just. So.

And, the "I" is a word that refers to … what? Nothing! Non-Objective Being, appearing as the Consciousness-Presence, conceptualized as "I AM" But YOU are That which is PRIOR TO that "I AM" concept and even prior to the Consciousness-Knowingness Itself! YOU are Pure Being that does not know that it is. THIS is Nonduality… One-No-Other.

Your actual NON-conceptual Being is not an object with properties therefore It cannot be attained, described or defined. See that clearly right now and the search is done.

Clear Seeing Is Naked And Open

Q: I love your no nonsense approach to nonduality. I am able to see that I am the Awareness in which everything appears, but only when I'm not caught up in all my miserable stories. Witnessing enables me to drop the stories. I don't yet see that I am everything that appears in the Awareness that I Am. It kind of sounds like I'm emptying the mirage cup. Namaste.

C: It's nice to hear from you my friend. Namaste' back! Good "seeing" happening there ... but to set the record right that reference to the mirage was in a quote I posted written by John Wheeler ... http://beingisknowing.blogspot.com/2009/10/this-weeks-quote.html (from www.thenaturalstate.org).

Now, let's have a look: We say "I don't see yet that I am everything". What is that "I" that claims to "see or not see"? What is it really? Just an arising thought, appearing in awareness. The suffering kicks in when we take that one-letter-word, "I", to be what we are. That single core concept is the imaginary self, the falsely believed reference point. And as Bob Adamson tells us that all suffering is self-centered conceptualizing. Seeing is happening. Then we take it to be true that "I" see (or I don't see). Getting down to brass tacks, IS that "I" anything solid at all? Or isn't that ONLY a passing thought that is not always so, where the Awareness IS always so?

Notice how we attempt to take on a "new enlightened identity" by claiming "I am awareness". The pointer is that yes, what you and I really are IS awareness. But the concept is NOT the actual naked awareness. This is a subtle point that the mind misses because the mind is a mechanism that grasps, defines and claims to be some thing; even some "huge thing" like "everything". But those are all concepts, and YOU are NOT ANY concept!

When it gets pointed out that our true identity is undefined and undefineable; that NO definition can describe or represent who we are, then the mind can get very frustrated...because it MUST have a definition. That is its nature. So it takes on the "nondual identity" (how's THAT for an oxymoron!) called "I AM

AWARENESS. The old saying, "I am consciousness and bliss, I am Shiva, I am Shiva" is just another identity and ANY identity is untrue and unreal. The Reality pointed to as Nondual is NOT a concept, so any identity will become a fixation and it is that fixation that is right at the very heart or our human suffering. Rooting out that core comes in understanding that this "me" or "I" is ONLY a thought that comes and goes in naked awareness.

Can a thought be reality? Can something that is not permanent be truly real? No. This is why the pointer comes out, "you are no thing". And a thought, any thought, is clearly a thing, isn't it?

ANY identity is temporary and nothing more than a thought while awareness, presence, open and clear, is no thought, no thing, and That Thou Art ... identity-less!

Staying with the clarity of this potent understanding provides the heat and light necessary to melt away the cloud of ignorance. As Sri Nisargadatta said, "understanding is all". Self-knowledge is the only cure for self ignorance ...ignorance means ignoring the real and favoring the false sense of being a "me". Seeing and knowing that awareness is never absent is self-knowledge. But this seeing is not of the "person" ... there is no person in reality. The knowing is sans knower ... this is simply naked seeing, naked knowing.

This is why it is said, in Dzogchen: The great perfection is non-conceptual, ever-fresh, self-shining, presence-awareness, just this and nothing else.

Glad to hear from you any time. Stay in touch and feel free to write here or to non.duality@yahoo.com if any more questions or doubts about your True nature of Non-conceptual Being-Awareness arise. All doubts are self-centered conceptualization arising in present naked awareness, and you were never any concept!

You Are Unborn. Full stop.

A Challenge To The Fictional "Me"

Stay with facts; reject false assumptions.

What you are is a FACT. The sense of Being, Presence, the knowingness "I AM" is simply beyond dispute. Abide as I AM and the imaginary problems fade out... It is said, THAT, I AM, Thou Art ("Tat Tvam Asi"). The wholeness that You Truly Are is nothing but this ever-fresh Knowing, I AM. Full Stop! Your Real Self is Unborn Awareness ... Awareness is never born and never dies ... Awareness is the Changeless Reality Itself. You Are THAT.

What we point out is that the root cause must be ELIMINATED. Seeing the mechanism is a first step, for sure. But to challenge the mind's assertions of belief until that cause is DISMANTLED is what is said to be the "means"... "Give up all questions except, Who Am I?" And, "Refuse all thoughts except, I Am." ~ Sri Nisargadatta Maharaj

"The thought 'who am I?' will destroy all other thoughts, and like the stick used for stirring the burning pyre, it will itself in the end get destroyed. Then, there will arise Self-realization." ~ Sri Ramana Maharshi

The point is, if any suffering remains, it has NOT been fully exposed and dismantled! Where IS the "I" that makes THIS claim? Who says that suffering has been exposed? This claim is made by an ego that resists being REALLY seen and dismantled! Keep looking, dig down and locate the real Source of the I thought; that one thought "I" is the fixative and the fixation, the "glue" is that energy of belief going into a false self center that on earnest and committed investigation simply cannot be found! Root out that cause and the effects die on the vine of True Seeing.

Start from the one FACT you are certain of: I AM. Look for the SOURCE of this I AM-NESS that you know is so. No one can tell you, you are not. That sense of presence, of Existingness, is all you know by direct knowing rather than conceptualizing. Suffering can only consist and persist in conceptualizing self as a separate suffering thing ... "poor me", "woe is me", etc. Get real with this. Suffering is optional!

(Later)

Q: It couldn't be more obvious that the 'I' thought has no root or cause. That's been obvious for some 'time'. It's also been obvious that all there is is this, that is, what's currently manifesting.

C: I don't buy that. If it's really seen that way, there would be NO suffering!

Q: All else (i.e., thought) is an illusion and suggests past, preset, future, etc. Of course all appears now. Yes, you can not say that you are not and that is it. It is so simple and obvious.

C: So where is the problem? And for whom is there a problem?

Q: I agree that "if any suffering remains, it has NOT been fully exposed and dismantled!"

C: Please: DON'T AGREE or DISAGREE. LOOK INTO THIS for yourself!

Q: But who is to expose or dismantle it?

C: That "you" that still says I, I am this person, I still suffer. That "you" that is only a passing idea, energy-sound in Awareness, yet that idea is being taken to be real. To be "you!" Challenge that! Don't just buy into some "nondual platitude" like "there is no one so who will look"? That is a ploy the ego-ideation uses to avoid its own being outed as the fake it really is. The emperor doesn't want to be found out to have no clothes. YOU are Naked Awareness. Any idea to the contrary needs to be investigated and dismantled. The search began in the mind so the challenge to our cherished assumption of "I am I, Me" MUST be taken on IN that very mind. This is a paradox to the mind that wants the security of an answer. The "Answer" there is no one will still leave you suffering, as you are admitting when you are being honest about your actual experience. In my experience the structure of conceptualizing consists in A) interpretations of what is, including judgments and evaluations of what "should be different" or "could be better" that what simply IS, B) the fixation that "what is appearing is a real happening and it's all happening to ME, and C) the core assumption that I AM the THOUGHT-BELIEF I, Me, My Self in a World Out There which I am separate from, and D) there IS a location for ME and there is also TIME, a past and future, which constrains ME.

Q: What can I say??? This character continues to 'suffer' in numerous ways. I can only think that it is the constant coming back or staying with what already is that can end this suffering. But, is ("me") ready for that? I don't see how he ever could be.

C: Clearly if you are looking at this you ARE ripe and ready. Just finish it

Q: What do you mean by dismantled?

C: To see what is false about "you" … to deconstruct that house of cards by getting underneath the assumed isness of a "person" (the persona, or mask) by deeply investigating what is real and what is unreal. ANYTHING that comes and goes is UNREAL. Is that much understood?

Q: Do you mean resting as your true self moment to moment, untouched by anything in manifestation or un-manifestation?

C: NO! You are ALREADY That ... untouched Being. To try to "rest as that" is dualism ... it creates a false division between That and "one who would rest as That". This is faulty logic! Who cannot see that what you always already ARE is empty, meaningless Being-Knowing Awareness Itself? Get UNDER the assumption "I am Me"!

Q: Of course, that's always the case. Again, what can be said? 'Some' appear to have dismantled … Others appear to be chasing their own tails.

C: Exactly where are those "others"? Only in your mind! Your assumption of being a separate person drives a false perception/assumption "there are others out there who are NOT "me"; some "special persons" who have "attained some state". That is all bullshit, a product of an inaccurate perspective. All perspectives are false: what You Are is No-Perspective, No-

Location, No-Time, just Being. No more or less than Being Itself.

Q: Calling it a 'cosmic joke' could not be more appropriate!

C: On who? On the false concept of a self that cannot be found!

Q: I would also say that a process of 'dying' is occurring - I just wish that it would hurry up! LOL. Of course, that's just another belief, albeit, a rather attractive one.

C: No process is needed for you to BE, as You Are ... this bare presence-awareness.

Q: What would be real is getting beyond the words of it and actually living it, moment to moment forever and ever. The words also chase their own tails!

C: WHO? WHO makes these claims or wants what is not already here right now? WHO!?

Q: Nevertheless, it's so purifying to bathe in the clarity of one's own self (self recognizing self)...

C: That is just another "spiritual belief. What needs to be "purified"? Does your Being need purification?

No.

That is already utterly pure, open and naked. You are just stuck in some spiritual or psychological concepts which have NO inherent validity whatsoever.

Take it all apart.

Get really curious to actually understand the mechanics of your mental suffering. Dismantling the ego-assumption may APPEAR to be a "process" in "time" but you can see right now that it's all a story told by a storyteller that is no more than imagination.

See what's REAL and take apart what's false... that's the job the mind must do to dismantle itself. Paradoxically.

Get down under the false beliefs and assumptions; seek the SOURCE of the "I" assumption. When you find there is nothing there your questions and assumptions can no longer trouble you.

As Sri Nisargadatta said, "All that can trouble you is your own imagination". Find out for yourself if that is TRUE. In my experience, I KNOW that to be absolutely true.

That natural knowing came from looking deeply into this. I encourage you to get after it and resolve these issues for your self...and I mean Right Now.

Pointers From No One To No Where

What is absolutely present and aware, right here, right now? You are That. No One. No Where. Now Here.

Who are you? Whatever That is, is it changing? Is it moving? Is it a "thing" at all? If That which is Always So, always Shining before the next thought appears, is not a "thing" then what is it? Who can say what That really IS? Who would dare to divide God into pieces; the Singular I into two? I and other? How dare we limit God, our Self? Who do we think we are to believe such nonsense? Find out.

No matter what appears, it appears now. When? Now. Where? Here.

What is, IS. Apparently! What is not, is NOT. Immaculately.

Now and then are both imagination.

Who do you think you are? Whatever that is, You are Not That.

There is no time like this presence. There is no place like Home.

Wherever the body goes, it is Here ... Haven't You noticed? What is this "Here" that IS?

You are not what you know. You are not even what you don't know.

All words are lies. That's the Truth! (NOT)

Do you know what is eternal? How do you know anything? Isn't there That Obviously Aware Presence, wherever you are? Whatever the clock might display?

How do you know what you think or believe you know? How do you know that you know that you know? What is That which you don't know that you don't know?

Disagreements Are Only "In The Mind"

Q: One thing I would like to discuss is all the apparent disagreement between teachers in their way of presenting this. As a seeker, teachers disagreeing with one another was a horrific thing, because it made my advaita world get a little bit shaky underfoot. (Solid rock turned out to be quicksand!) None of this is a problem if there's no seeker, but for someone trying to get down and dirty with this, as I was, it seemed like I had to forget what everyone had ever said to me, ever. Even while I was with Tony, there was the notion of "Don't even worry about the words he's saying, just get right in there and look." So much time seemed to be into trying to tweak these concepts, and get hits of power from those pointed out the real. Is that sort of how it was for you? A sort of throwing overboard of all the stuff, and just getting really raw with the thing? Thanks a lot for your thoughts, all the best.

C: You wrote, ".... Don't even worry about the words he's saying, just get right in there and look."

Yes, the words are ultimately irrelevant, BUT ... the identity is language so without language pointing, the looking won't happen. Now, you ask "how did it happen for 'you'?" That ignores the fact that Awareness is what is real and the 'you' is an appearance IN Awareness. Can an appearance "have something happen" for it? It is JUST an appearance. Nail that down or the expression can be a bit off the mark...

As far as the 'teacher war', well, that is all the show, isn't it? It has no intrinsic meaning; the mind is a "me-making and meaning-making machine". Looking for the source of the machinery, with a gentle yet persistent curiosity about "what makes the machinery run on believing it is a real separate I?" is usually what is called for. In my view, starting from the FACT (sans speculation or description) that Being IS and That is what is real, and knowing yourself as THAT, as simple naked awareness, is the gate. Going through the gate is a happening that appears as part of the show ... an apparent 'happening' IN that Being, that Awareness. But appearance is forever changing so nothing in the changing show can be trusted! None nada zip.

So drop all the battles over who says what right. It cannot be said right! Yet when the sharing is coming from Source it has an unmistakable flavor to the heart. That is kind of what I listen for. I have many links posted, because regardless of the words there is a sense of aliveness-source permeating. Some who are coming from duality and posing as "teachers" don't make the cut! Anyways, there is no problem with anything except the mind makes it so and NO one is that mind. Everything is JUST the show... but only Everything!

And The Show and The Screen of Awareness ON which The Show appears are …

NOT TWO.

Nuff said!

You Are Unborn. Full stop.

Row row row your boat

gently down the stream

merrily merrily merrily merrily

life is but a dream...

Only naked awareness is real.

All else is the dream.

"The Basics" Of This

1. YOU are Awareness, simply being. No one can say they do not exist. That existence, the sense of "I" as in "I Am," is undeniable and inescapable. Try to NOT BE. Cannot be done. So the simple pointer is, what you are is That Presence of Awareness .In short: YOU ARE. That's IT. Being. Just That! This True You ... BE-ING... is POINTED TO in language with concepts like Impersonal Consciousness; Awareness, Being ... YOU are just THAT, prior to the mind's translation into the thought I Am and I am this or that.

2. You are NOT an "individual." There are NO "individuals" anywhere except in unreal stories. The idea of a separate person is a fiction, a mind-construction, a house of cards, as the story tries to say, "I'm ME! (Unsuccessfully!) This idea of a "me" is ... on investigation ... seen to be a false claim by the thinking machinery to its own separate existence. This ever-changing idea of a person is simply unreal. WHO says "I'm Me?" The mind. To be blunt, it's bullshit. The whole fabricated story of me is pure bullshit: all stories of "individuals" is actually a fiction. As Shakespeare said, it's a tale told by an idiot, filled with sound and fury, signifying ... NOTHING.

Look right now! Seeing with naked Awareness, where is any person ... unless you (as a mind-identity) think about it? Thoughts come and go. What you ARE NEVER comes and goes anywhere. It is (You Are) fully Here Now and Eternally Free and Clear, Eternally Presence, Shining before the mind.

YOU are not a thought, not a concept, not a feeling, not a time bound entity. You are Awakeness, Aliveness, Presence-Awareness. Just THAT and NOTHING else. The story of "me" ... ANY "me" ... is irrelevant. Let's cut through that crap right now! Okay?

Let's bring this back to the basics: What in YOU never changes? Being-Awareness, just That. That is your True Nature. The Ultimate Subject IN which and AS which all apparent "objects" appear.

Where is a separate entity when you are in deep dreamless sleep? Or under anesthesia? There is none. Obviously! But some Presence beats the heart, breathes air in and out, flows the blood, grows new cells and disintegrates other cells, grows hair and fingernails, ages the body etc etc! Who or what is "doing" all that? Not an "individual," "amazing" or otherwise.

Look and see that you are present and aware right now. That is the "Eternal," The Natural State"; there is no other, no attainment, no flashy enlightened state, no carrot on a stick. There is NO someday when "you" will "get enlightened." It's what you are right now. There is no other than NOW. Wherever you are you are ... Here. That's IT. Big Casino. You already got it in total and there's nothing more to this Nonduality stuff than that simple seeing, that you ARE. Awareness, Simply That.

Stay with facts; reject false assumptions

What you are is a FACT. The sense of Being, Presence, the knowingness "I AM" is simply beyond dispute. Abide as I AM and the imaginary problems fade out... It is said, THAT, I AM, Thou Art ("Tat Tvam Asi"). The wholeness that You Truly Are is nothing but this ever-fresh Knowing, I AM. Full Stop.

Scared Crows and Scary Scarecrows

I recently saw a TV show where there was a cornfield, in the middle of which was a "well dressed scarecrow". A straw man in second hand K-mart clothes.

What does a scarecrow do? Does "he" scare off the crows, thereby protecting the crop from hungry winged vandals? If you think so I have a bridge in New York City that I'd like to sell you!

For the crows, the scarecrow is a real person in that cornfield, standing tall and scary looking, a "someone" who threatens their existence, so they steer clear of "him". But that is the CROW'S perspective, a programmed response to an imaginary threat taken to be real because the crow cannot discriminate between the appearance of a thing and Reality of that appearance.

Are most "humans" any different? Are YOU any different? Do you cross the street when a group of unruly looking teenagers is headed your way? Does your heart beat a little quicker, your breath get a little shallow? Does the body tense up? Then welcome to Crow World, where nothing is as it seems and everything is how it is perceived, through crow-colored glasses.

Aren't we like that, so long as there is the conviction that we are "persons" and can by consequence of that false conviction, be threatened by other "persons"? What if that is all simply projection, a perception colored by crow-tinted glasses, and NOT really real?

Now look: I am NOT saying, "don't cross the street if the body feels that it is threatened" But I AM saying, notice the mechanism of assuming "those kids over there are dangerous and they are people with free will who may hurt ME."

The me is the only problem. When that "me" is no more, there remains nothing that can ever be threatened. The Original Self that You really ARE is No Thing. How can No Thing be threatened? Only things can be threatened; only things can die or be hurt or born or know irrational fear.

When the "me" is deconstructed there is only I AM-ness, the unborn, appearing as a body-mind. That bodymind will act in accordance with its programming, and that may include crossing the street or locking your door. But that will be naturally happening in the moment; what is gone forever when there is no longer that false belief in the "me-person", when that mask (persona) has dropped into the nowhere from which it appeared temporarily, then there is no longer that "secondary involvement" with it's mental gymnastics about "concern for survival" (if I don't cross the street what will happen to me? If I do will I be safe or will that gang chase me?)

So crossing the street happens, and there is no secondary chatter about what if this or what if that. Then perhaps you see the group from across the street as they pass on the other side and it becomes obvious that these are nice kids from your own block, and the imagined threat goes poof.

The metaphor in this is pointing only to the actual, factual, non-existence of any person, in the scarecrow, OR in that organism you might call "yourself". When this is seen to be that case, whether that seems to happen spontaneously or through some apparent "doing" on your part (asking "Who Am I?", for example) all such secondary involvement just disappears and life is lived in freedom, fearlessly and effortlessly.

So notice if there is this kind of irrational self-centered secondary involvement, and pull the plug on it. Perhaps in talking to one who sees what is real, and perhaps though reading, or perhaps just because it happens all by itself the actual happening is causeless despite appearances... regardless, that plug pulling ends suffering in the Eternal Now ... and that is "a consummation devoutly to be wished... "

THAT is the real death of this "me" which was never born; leaving That Which Always IS... You as Your Self.

Don't Miss The Simplicity Of This Reality

Something sees these letters and sees the forms called words, and that same ever-present something sees the space between the letters and the words, the screen of the computer or blank page that allows these marks to appear, and the space in which computer or book, the body, the knower-seer, are all arising out of nowhere (now here). That Space of Being Awareness effortlessly holds and allows it all to be as it is. No resistance. Eternally Presencing Reality.

Did you overlook all these spaces and the Space-Awareness that allows it all to appear? Right here and now are you overlooking the Being-Presence that allows the seeing of the body? The observing of the I thought that appears? What is seeing? Being sees and sees the appearance of a self, reading. That Being is what You are. It takes NO time or effort to BE. This, Being-Eternally-existing, is what you are.

Don't believe the voice in your head that tells you that you are a thing that can suffer and die. Being as you are means abandoning all identities once and forever. You are That - Being, and nothing else.

What Happens in Investigating This "me"?

It could be said that the only "purpose" of the seeking mind to "self-inquire" is to discover once and for all that it will never "work". As that event (which might be called "Grace") happens, it becomes absolutely clear that the mind, the "ego-sense we call 'me'," CAN NEVER "know itself" as Being beyond itself!

Being is incontrovertible, inescapable and non objective; the only "separation" from Being that ever happened or could happen is in language only, and language is dreamlike, insubstantial and powerless. There is no way out of Being and no way to attain Being. To "attain" requires "don't already have" and THAT is the false identification with a movement of Divine Energy ... we call that movingness a thought ... of an "I"... which we have made solid and real in our inadvertence and ignorance; The assumption of a separate "me" is JUST an assumption.

There is just flat NO evidence that "you" are separated from "me". All there IS, is THIS ... whatever is apparently happening is NO thing appearing as all that is.

So the seeking and inquiry or meditation or any other seeker-practices go on by themselves (though we falsely claim to being doing them!) until the absolute futility is finally recognized and the mind just dies on the vine of Being-The-Absolute, timelessness is revealed and the false self center is obliterated.

And in THAT there is clear seeing that there never was any substantiality to the "me" ... it was only a dreamed character appearing in Oneness' Dream of Being Two!

So whatever you do as a doer will never work. There is no way out of Being and no way to attain what already always IS. Seeing this (which no one sees!) ends the seeking and all there is, is ALL there IS. This. Is. It.

Test this out, though! Do the work. If one simply gives up and gets resigned, believing that there is nothing to do and no one to do it, that belief is just anther delusion: sounds good to the mind that fights against being investigated and found to be a charlatan, but that belief is just another clever ploy the mind will use to avoid being "outed" as the fake it really is!

Do NOT believe any of this. Please. The only test for truth is in your own patient and earnest investigation of what seems real but is not real and never was real.

Do the work; find out what is false, the believed-in "persona", the mask the mind has developed in innocence and ignorance, the false assumption that is the root of suffering, and the Truth appears and is seen by no one to be what is Always So.

Your True Self is hiding in plain sight. Your True Self is … everything. But ONLY Everything.

This Is It - NOT

There is nothing hidden, no secret, and nothing special for the fictional "person" to attain.

There is no "someday when", no "future enlightenment", no "awakening", no "liberation," no "energy contraction", no "explosion into Oneness".

All that stuff is a story, the "tale told by an idiot, signifying nothing!"

What is "IT"? Not this. Not this. Any "this" that can be said? It's not. Not this not this not this. Then what? THAT. YOU are THAT, not this not this just THAT…..

As Sri Nisargadatta pointed out in "I Am That", the TRUE Guru is your own Self. It is only He that will take you to the goal, because He (She) IS the goal. It is absolutely TRUE that You are already what you seek, and seeking that truth is the denial OF that truth.

So maybe the Guru lied if he or she said you are not already That, not already whole and complete. Look into it. Find out what is real … for yourself. Take no one else's word for any of it. Believe nothing. Investigate!

The transcendent Understanding (note the capital U) is simply this: You are NOT an "individual." There are NO "individuals" anywhere except in unreal stories. The idea of a separate person is a fiction, a mind-construction, a house of cards, as the story tries to say, "I'm ME! (Unsuccessfully!) This idea of a "me" is be a false claim ... an assertion devoid of authentic evidence ... made by a machine, linguistic machinery ... to it's own separate existence. This ever-changing idea of a person is simply unreal. WHO says "I'm Me?" The mind. To be blunt, it's bullshit. The whole fabricated story of me is pure bullshit: all stories of "individuals" is actually a fiction. As Shakespeare said, it's a tale told by an idiot, filled with sound and fury, signifying ... NOTHING. It's all made up ... by no one!

Where is there any "person"? The "person" is merely a

temporary appearance that arises ONLY in "thoughts", subtle words, language. Thoughts come and go. What you ARE NEVER comes and goes anywhere. It is (You Are) fully Here Now and Eternally Free and Clear, the One Eternal Presence.

Look and see that there IS BEING. Being IS, Being is Eternally No Thing, BEING IS, even before the mentally constructed temporal notions of "here" or "now".

BEING IS. Just THAT as-it-is- not.

There is NO someday when "you" will "get enlightened." It's what you are right now. There is no other than THAT. BEING IS. One Not Two. No Thing appearing as everything. There is nowhere else, there is no one else; there is ONLY BEING. ONLY Not This. As It IS....

This Is It. NOT. That is all there is.

Just THAT and Nothing Else.

As Bob Adamson puts is, THAT is One Essence Appearing As Everything.

And That's That.

"Seeker of truth, follow no path; all paths lead where; the truth is Here"

ee cummings.

Who Sez?

As is said many places, you are what you seek. And if liberation does not come from the Source itself, which is your Original Nature, then where will it arise from?

Can "you" do anything to attain what you already are? Isn't that a fool's errand? Can you get Here from Here?

What was born? Was a "me" or a "you" ever real as a separate "designer of life"?

Look at all that happens ... see if you can locate any entity writing a script for the dance of the kazillions of particles in this manifest appearance? If there comes to arise a profound gift of Unearned Grace ... then perhaps the notion of egoic assumptions of any real control will wither and die. But no one can either "cause" or "prevent" that "happening".

The phantom writer of this life opera cannot erase itself. There is no one anywhere to do that. Not you, not your guru, not any "other" than the one Life Itself.

Life appears and then you seem to be needed for life to happen, and you say life happens "to me", "for me". Is that true?

Who says so?

It Is WAY Too Simple

Do you "know yourself as a person", as "someone seeking" wholeness, oneness, liberation" or some other imaginary "enlightenment"?

Let's be clear. There will never be any "enlightenment" for the identity, the fixated entity, simply owing to the fact (FACT) that there IS no fictional person. But that is not a "truth" … it is only a pointer to ponder if you like, to perhaps prompt the deeper insight. This occurs … or NOT … all by itself. IF Investigation happens, done by no one, as a functioning of the Wholeness of the Nondual Essence. Though no one is "doing" or "authoring" that investigation it MAY happen and there MAY be the direct seeing, a sudden dropping of the mask of "me" so to say. But there is no way the "me" can cause that. So one might call the arising of that … Grace.

Can a character in a film running on the TV "get enlightened"? It may appear so because of the script that the author put on the page for the actor to follow … like say, "The Razor's Edge", supposedly about a seeker who traveled to India to meet Ramana Maharshi and "got it". But it's a MOVIE!

And in THIS "movie called my life" in which "I" is the star, and seems also to be the writer, producer and director … it is NO different: We are being "acted" by Source, or God, or IS, or whatever label you like that doesn't get rejected out of the mind's programmed sense of it's own superiority to any such greater Being. So, the movie and players appearing and the nondual essence of innate naked perfectness are TWO aspects of ONE … Consciousness appearing as Is and Is Not … a single whole we "label" (perhaps) "Nondual perfection".

It is a story that is forever told by the fixated persona and the fictional "masters" that simply never comes true for the individuated consciousness called "me".

Yet the happening of a Guru, a Teaching, or some other functioning of Infinite Isness may arise. Great good fortune, beyond any notion of cause and effect. Beyond volition, beyond predestination, beyond free will, beyond both being and non-being ... the happening of Final Seeing for no one. Empty mind, Heart fills, and Life lives on through the organism. BUT: There is NO "cause-effect relationship" for that occurring. The Guru does NOT enlighten anyone. Yet the Guru may be a window, then a door, through which The One Essence appears to act. But "cause and effect" are a story with NO basis in reality! It is said in many ways, all is the functioning of a Totality which simply CANNOT be known, explained, or understood by an intellect! And yet, there is a natural Being-Knowing that is prior to all stories that arises from the Eternal Being that you are. And stuff still happens. So what? Bodhi Svaha.

There IS Peace. There IS Understanding. There IS "enlightenment" But not so long as you are there.

You are NOT what you KNOW you are.

Ordinary Seeing

The seeker mind cannot see that while it says "I want spiritual liberation", that is ACTUALLY the very LAST thing the seeker REALLY wants. This naked, ordinary and obvious seeing is the "death of a thing never born". Oxymoronically speaking!

This Being-knowing doesn't belong to anyone. No one was ever born who needs liberation from the ego, dissolution of the false, deconstruction of the false sense of 'me', or any other so-called spiritual enlightenment. YOU are already freedom, life itself. How can something that never existed in the first place attain some state of peace for itself?

Who cannot see the oxymoron in that assumption of a 'me' who will 'become whole' in an imaginary 'someday-other-than-right-now'? The seeker seeks itself, chasing its tail.

This goes on until it doesn't! OR, until the seeker takes up an investigation into what is false and what is REAL.

This Being-Seeing-Experiencing is so alive, so present, and so utterly intimately non-conceptual, that concepts cannot ever approach this Thus-ness and Such-ness of what IS.

The air conditioning caresses my skin, loving to ease the heat. Oneness caresses your identity in Love and that is ultimate intimacy, inescapably you are you.

All there is is YOU, called either 'you' or 'not-you'. So what? So nuthin'.

What's for dinner?

Naked and Obvious

Ben Franklin may have said, "The truth is self-evident.... malice may attack it; ignorance may deride it, but in the end, there it is".

Yes. HERE, It Is.

The naked truth of Being is self-evident. Being IS and the Truth is You ARE That ... simply Being.

There is ONLY BEING.

Life Itself, The Livingness, Infinite Unbounded Knowing-Aliveness.

Full on, balls to the wall, Aliveness!

There is nothing more to Nonduality than this ... You know with zero doubt, "I AM". Yes?

WHAT that I AM is, one cannot say. I AM is no more or less than ordinary, naked awareness, fully present at every moment of Now, fully awake, whole, and alive, The One.

That is NOT a concept; it is direct ... nowhere and everywhere.

You Are That. You are Being, Unborn, Free.

You ARE ... and That is ... the One Absolute.

There is NO Other that That.

This Is Nearly Impossible To Communicate

How can "your eternal Unborn True-Nature" be communicated so "you" can get it and know it?

That is patently IMPOSSIBLE!

"What?" I hear you shout: "You have written books, you have a blog and other websites, all certainly purporting to communicate possibilities for freedom etc. How dare you?!"

Fair enough! It is a fine question, but you might not like the answer. The bottom line is what you are can NOT be communicated EVER. Never! Why? Because there simply IS NO YOU to receive and there is no other to send!

This Reality is uncommunicable. Communication requires separation, a you and an other. And THAT is the irresolvable dilemma that arises in language (and ONLY in language).

Well then, how is it that all these books etc. happen? The straight answer from the "person-called-charlie" is, I DO NOT KNOW! In fact no books exist, there's no writer or reader anywhere, the whole thing is a big fat dream!

Without language, where is an "IS"? book, an IS writer, an IS reader? Where or what is a you or other without language? And how can a phantom discover it is a phantom? How can a dream character "become self-realized?" the dream character DOES NOT EXIST. How can a "thing" that does not exist "discover" it's NON-existence?

The whole world is language. Is language, which is all concepts, actually a Real "reality?" Where is tomorrow yesterday today without language? Is the word water WET?

The answer is WAY too simple for the mind. It is just this: You do NOT exist! All there is, is language … and No Thing.

Language appears to be real in its own innocent ignorance. But it's NOTHING. Language is a self-creating delusion, a self-referring entitification-machine with absolutely no ACTUAL "Isness" at all. In short it is the Big Joke Oneness plays on itself by Being and bullshitting itself by languaging until it doesn't.

Laughter happens!

But if you are that you are you, you will not laugh because Oneness-being-language has made YOU the butt of this JOKE.

Often when "people" encounter that, they get REALLY PISSED OFF.

BUT THAT AIN'T Real Either! It's ALL language. ALL story. ALL bullshit.

So called nonduality "teachers" are teaching BULLSHIT to themselves and think that there some "other" out there listening. Obviously that cannot "work". It's like a farmer growing mushrooms: You keep them in the dark and feed them bullshit.

So to say words that are just more bullshit, you are Oneness doing this to yourself, BUT there IS no you so what-are-ya-gonna-do?

What is who gonna do?

This really IS hopeless!

Yet Oneness seems to keep on tilting at windmills until it doesn't.

Or until there comes into the Hands Of Oneness masked as a "human", some pointers that empower a new kind of looking and seeing … a seeing of what is Real and a dismantling of what is unreal.

That is Grace. AKA really good luck!

So this is impossible to communicate, AND communication happens. No one doing it, yet the happening appears.

The profound paradoxical mystery of Being, Unborn.

How cool is that!?

Who? Who? WHO?

A question arrived one day... quite a common question: The seeker wanted to know, if it is true that there is actually no person, then who is doing the investigation?

The simple answer is, who investigates the false, at first, is that very "self" you assume exists, as evidenced by your asking this. It's that idea of a "you" that asked this question. That's where it starts: The search for wholeness began in this mind-construct and must be addressed there, at least in "early days." This is why we often say; look at WHO is asking this question? The question arises ... but is there a question-ER? Who or what IS that if there is one? Can you find a subject-questioner of an object-question? Or NOT? Be honest!

The seeker responded, "When I look in the way suggested, I find nothing and nobody."

Right, there IS nobody to answer the question; the mind is checkmated by the question! Yet in the next breath, the same seeker asks again, well, then, WHO is doing the inquiry? Okay, the "ultimate answer" is, Totality asks itself who am I and on finding no answer, gives up the question, the door swings open, and the seeker is blown through by Love into Love. But early on that may just be another lofty concept to the mind that thinks it is NOT The One Self of All, and so frustration can grow here big time!

Asked and answered! But no answer satisfies the mind's search because in the final Truth there IS no answer. THAT is the "answer!" So the admonition comes, well, keep looking until that No-Answer, No-Body, is more solid and real than any thought of a "me" ... or other apparent "obstruction".

Yet this IS a paradox of great magnitude ... but only to the conditioned mind. Paradox is two opposing concepts. The conflict is resolved in the clear seeing that NO concept could ever fit the only cogent definition of the Real: That which NEVER changes. What never changes where you appear right now? Are you awake? Awakeness is unchanging in the waking state. Are you aware? Awareness never changes in ANY state (though "consciousness" comes and goes, the Awareness-Light of Truth is always shining regardless of whether there is consciousness or not.)

Things are getting snarky now, right? This loop-de-loop is where things can get confusing, because on investigation no separate and real "individual" is anywhere to be found, that alone cannot satisfy the habitual mind-pattern that is so accustomed to its false beliefs that a cursory or superficial challenge is rarely sufficient to accomplish the (apparent) de-construction of this edifice built on the I-concept.

The I has gotten added to, since language happened in the very young brain, and the first add-on is "I am this body." I am here as THIS thing and all that out there is NOT me. That assumption, and it is ONLY an assumption for which there is absolutely NO evidence, is the root cause of all apparent suffering, seeking, and endless questions that no answer stills for good.

So when the seeker says, "I find nobody", that is a major insight! The Self IS No-Body. Not body, Not thought, Not feeling, Not any thing at all.

If there is still a struggle with this paradoxical sharing that yes, Virginia, there IS NO Santa Claus ... yes, there is no person apart from totality, AND so long as YOU think, believe or know yourself to BE such due to long practiced habitual lying to oneself about what we know as true, then absolutely investigation is called for.

The most powerful way to look I ever found (before meeting John Wheeler) came from Bhagavan Ramana Maharshi in the little book, "The Spiritual Teachings of Sri Ramana Maharshi". The first and most on point chapter is called "Nan Yar" ... or "Who Am I?"

For those who want to truly get the investigation done once and for good, this one pointer can "do the job" of rooting out the only cause of psychological egoic suffering ... the belief "I am ME and separated from God or Source".

The essence of it is this:

Devotee: "What is the path of inquiry for understanding the nature of the mind?

Bhagavan: That which rises as 'I' in this body is the mind. If one inquires as to where in the body the thought 'I' rises first, one would discover that it rises in the heart. That is the place of the mind's origin. Even if one thinks constantly 'I' 'I', one will be led to that place. Of all the thoughts that arise in the mind, the 'I' thought is the first. It is only after the rise of this that the other thoughts arise. It is after the appearance of the first personal pronoun that the second and third personal pronouns appear; without the first personal pronoun there will not be the second and third.

D: How will the mind become quiescent?

B: By the inquiry 'Who am I?'. The thought 'who am I?' will destroy all other thoughts, and like the stick used for stirring the burning pyre, it will itself in the end get destroyed. Then, there will arise Self-realization.

D: What is the means for constantly holding on to the thought 'Who am I?'

B: When other thoughts arise, one should not pursue them, but should inquire: 'To whom do they arise?' It does not matter how many thoughts arise. As each thought arises, one should inquire with diligence, "To whom has this thought arisen?" The answer that would emerge would be "To me". Thereupon if one inquires "Who am I?" the mind will go back to its source; and the thought that arose will become quiescent.

With repeated practice in this manner, the mind will develop the skill to stay in its source. When the mind that is subtle goes out through the brain and the sense-organs, the gross names and forms appear; when it stays in the heart, the names and forms disappear. Not letting the mind go out, but retaining it in the Heart is what is called "inwardness" (antar-mukha). Letting the mind go out of the Heart is known as "externalization" (bahir-mukha).

110

Thus, when the mind stays in the Heart, the 'I' which is the source of all thoughts will go, and the Self which ever exists will shine. Whatever one does, one should do without the egoity "I". If one acts in that way, all will appear as of the nature of Shiva (God)."

(Found on the public website, http://www.angelfire.com/realm/bodhisattva/whoami.html).

There is also a lot more on this in my book "From I Am to I Am, with Love". Visit www.theeternalstate.org for info on obtaining a copy for yourself, if you find that Spirit moves that to happen.

The True I, The True Self

Q: This might sound crazy but somewhere I know that I am missing Life itself by not allowing this knowledge to be fully present and totally lived ... this is the main suffering ... how can one stop pushing Life away when seen that this is what is happening?

C: All those words, all your questions, are intrinsically meaningless thoughts. Notice the unchanging I AM that they appear in. All that is temporal (temporary!). What never changes is what you are. That is Love, accepting all that appears on its own Face, the presence of awareness that IS right here right now. Just see what is fully alive, present, and knowing right now, right here, before the 'time', 'you, or 'charlie' concepts appear.

You are That which cannot be touched by any word or object. That is what we call being-knowing-love. Remember NO word is the actual! The word love is not Love. Love is WORDLESS yet lovingly allows any and all words, objects, appearances ... without judgment, unaffected ... as the wonderful Indian text, "The Bhagavad Gita", pointed out, That cannot be blown by wind, wetted by rain, burnt by fire. To know yourself as that requires the courage to give up all identification... all identities are false...reality is identity-less ... give up all ideas such as "I am this body with this name".

Know this for yourself, here and now: "Before God is, I AM."

Ask this also, who precisely IS this "I" that is "missing life itself by not allowing... etc" ... where is that separate I and is it actually a real thing apart? All the while you are claiming to be missing life, life is happening! Who cannot see this? There is nothing in the way of Life. If you believe you can alter anything in this dream of being in life itself, then stop the next hurricane from hitting Florida! It is our arrogance that claims we can "not allow" anything including realization that we are life itself. Drop it like the hot knife it is that seemingly murders your aliveness right now. All you have to lose is everything you hold dear... your imaginary limited self. Losing everything, the Paradise you never lost is "regained".

Q: To keep on pondering the jewels you gave here is what I feel is right as to respect their deep value... by now in investigation, no one is found as ever present I and at the same time I AM HERE... Who and where? No answer can ever actually fulfill the question... so the only thing that remain is the sense of being and the looking... Meet you in Paradise... Love You too in Freedom.

C: You say, "no one is found as ever present I and at the same time I AM HERE ..." that is the key insight! What is that I which is here now? The I Consciousness (A'Ham) ... endless beginningless Being. THAT I AM is true reality and love. Notice that THIS I AM is NOT a concept, NOT an idea, NOT even an experience! This I AM is the Paradise we were seeking ... stunningly finding It already fully present as this simple Being-Knowing-Loving.

So you have rediscovered Paradise in the simple seeing "there is no separate I and at the same eternal-time I AM." Here and now that I AM endures forever. You carry the whole universe here, in your own heart! I say welcome back to the Home you never left (the mind lied but now you know that Truth that sets us free in Itself. YAY!)

Another way to point ... the True I IS Ever-Present, Always ON ... in the same way that even when it appears to be dark outside we KNOW that the sun is ever-present, shining despite the appearance that it is not because the earth blocks the physical eye's view of it ... the knowing is naturally, the earth revolves around the sun and it is never not shining. But that was not obvious until Copernicus et al MADE it obvious by pointing out that what is real is, the sun does not move (and neither does Your Self). In this way see that the Light of Being, Awareness-Light, IS always shining and cannot be extinguished despite the appearance of thoughts, ideas and false beliefs that like the earth seems to keep the sun from view seem to keep the Light of the Eternal I from view. YOU are that Pure I that is seen here now; that is the Self of All. Know this now, don't refuse to be That, and don't pretend ever again you are not That.

That, I AM.

There is but ONE I-I BEING the knowing I AM.

This is the truth (satyam).

That Know-ING is The Truth that sets You free of 'you'.

Fear IS The "Me"

Q: I've watched some of your videos, along others from Tony Parsons, Jeff Foster, Unmani, and such... and I remembered a few hours ago that you're open to conversation by e-mail, so I thought I'd send you one...

C: Glad to hear from you!

Q: There has been this fear/anxiety/insomnia picking up in strength recently, particularly in the last two days, and there's really no way to end it or calm down when it picks up. I remember you in one of your videos saying that sometimes this whole thing is like making love to a 800 pounds gorilla: it ends when the gorilla's done!

C: Ha! Yes, and isn't it great that the gorilla (Oneness) is making LOVE and not WAR!

Q: I remember myself laughing when I heard that, but today the gorilla got more intense while I was at work, and it never happened like that before. I had to go to the bathroom because it was getting overwhelming and probably everyone around noticed just by looking at my face. So sometimes there's this fear, other times it's hopelessness, but there's like always that knot in the stomach. Inquiring into whose fear and anxiety this all is, well indeed I can't find anyone, and the inquiry tends to strengthen the knot.

C: It may SEEM to "strengthen the knot" but it is in fact LOOSENING the "knot" ... and in fact there IS no "knot" ... that's just a meaningless concept that does NOT represent any ACTUAL thing ... and what is plaguing you is nothing more than mental noise imagining a me and fear, overwhelm and other "problems for me" that are on deeper investigation NOT REAL. You are discovering that you truly can NOT find "anyone" yet the assumption is still operating, obviously, because that "fear" IS the false "me-persona!"

Q: Sometimes I'm having a hard time trying to find a point to self inquiry, since there's nothing to be found... but then I tell myself that "there's nothing to be found' is just some concept, and it's dropped. But then I might tell myself that it doesn't matter whether such non-dual concepts are dropped or not, because I'm just trying to find a way out after all, but a way out for what, and for whom? Etc... That's usually about how it goes when I self-inquire, I'm like chasing my tail it seems, and so it feels quite meaningless.

C: Yes, indeed it IS all meaningless, empty and unreal; the illusion of "me ... the mind must discover FOR ITSELF that there truly IS "no way out" and the final questions, "Who Am I?" and "Who asks this?" and "Who cares!?" are, for many, THE SOLVENT THAT DISSOLVES BELIEF IN A FALSE "ME". This false notion-emotion "I am me" is the root of all suffering; yet it's "deconstruction" may seem like an attack engendering fear. But, I repeat, that is ALL nothing more than empty, meaningless mental-emotional NOISE and at the heart absolutely unreal. So to share some good advice one of my teachers gave me, JUST KEEP GOING.

Q: So that's about it. I guess I'm sending this e-mail to you expecting that in some way you might help in bringing about some clarity, but there's this feeling of being vain at the same time. But anyway, I'll be glad to receive words from you.

C: Take on the bottom line challenge to your cherished assumptions, mainly the assumption "I am me" and "I am separate from others and the world". These assumptions are false but you (the brain-machine) must recognize this directly. The good news is you are on the precipice; that's why the energy arises of self survival. That survival mechanism is appropriate when naturally protecting the organism from impending harm ... if you inadvertently step in front of the bus, that mechanism will yank you back to the curb! But that mechanism has been co-opted by the falsely assumed self-centered identity and in this it is something that can be readily seen through as a kind of transparent con job Oneness plays on itself, so to speak! So in deeply allowing what appears to be and asking the questions, the fear dissolves back into the Timeless Love that it is actually made of; an energy of unconditional acceptance arises and the

116

false self falls off the fool's precipice and the search is done once and for good.

So, JUST KEEP GOING. Because even though there IS no person, the assumption that there is such must be dismantled directly by the brain that carries that virus of "me". So why not go for it!? Stay in touch if you like and remember, WHO YOU ARE is NOT a thing, not a changing assumed entity, NOT an "object", nothing the mind can grasp. Who says so? Who am I? WHAT am I? WHERE am I? Who is listening? WHO's watching the brain make these noises? Ask until there is no asker left and the Presence of Awareness that is the Unchanging Realty is clear and obvious (as it always is even now despite the brain noise that seems to deny that fact!) Much Love and all best wishes to you.

Q: Follow-up a while later ... Thanks so much for taking the time to answer the stupid questions you've probably heard a thousand times! In particular I seriously appreciate you calling me out on my wordy bullshit. I really needed it.

C: Good on ya! "From the beginning Not-A-Thing IS" :-) This is the end of "Becoming" and "Someday", isn't it? Much Love!

This Presence Of Awareness IS The Seeing

Q: Recently, I had a seeing I'd like to run by Presence to check the air pressure...am I over or under inflated?

C: Neither or both, take your pick, Puck!

Q: A thought occurred to me while I was sitting on the couch staring out the window. It was that none of what was being seen could be seen without thought.

C: Not true. Seeing thoughts is also Being, Seeing. There is always Consciousness-Seeing. Thought merely tries and fails to represent (RE Presence) what is already dead and gone so to say...

Q: All of what I was looking at were simply my mental projections. There was (and is) a direct seeing of this.

C: True in a way ... yet the moment it is described it is already past. The Presence of Awareness IS the Seeing, without a seer or seen which are just dead words, concepts. Meaningless to what IS. Yet that too is the pulsing of aliveness, energy, whatever label you like to put over label-less Being-Seeing-Knowing. This Knowing is NON-conceptual and yet, the brain "devolves" this to words which come and go in this Being-Reality You are. Underscoring this? You ARE and THAT is NOT A CONCEPT.

Q: When my brain dies, the world dies...I also had the same seeing with regard to the "story of Joe"...when thought dies, Joe dies. Too obvious for words. So, "me" and the world are just aggregates of thought, conditioning, opinions, memories...all to die when the organism dies.

C: The moment you say "I" or "MY" you are back into concepts. THIS is NON conceptual. Nothing being something being everything and THAT ain't a concept. It is not even an "IT". Words utterly FAIL here!

Q: The question then occurred to me, "what's left when all of these stories disappear?" An answer came to me...I have no idea! Words like presence, awareness, being mean nothing...there's just this unknowing...and a quietness, a total lack of any sense of urgency has settled over me...

C: Settles over whom? That natural joy and calm is the always-so background that seems (to the mind) to emerge through the membrane of identity as Oneness reveals Itself to Itself. But that story ain't true either! It's just a description of the Indescribable Isness of ALL this.

Q: I don't know if this makes sense, but there's just that unknowing and nothing else.

C: As a concept, YES. But remember NO concept is the Timeless Empty Joy of Being.

Q: There seems to be a great deal of peace in that unknowing. It appears to be a retelling of the great Cosmic Joke...the only thing you need to figure out is that there's nothing to figure out! I got this feeling that, "You're done. Now go live your life."

C: YES INDEED. But you don't live your life. Live lives YOU.

Q: Knowing of course that the I is just a mental construct...it can still be fun being "me" with a name and form.

C: Yep! The greatest joy there is, is the re-discovery of the natural statelessness which is for the human uncaused joy and absolute freedom. Then to pretend to be me all the while knowing naturally that it's ALL The Play Of Being. Timelessness appearing as time, form, all of this. Nothing is resisted and nothing is rejected OR accepted as there is no doer to do such erroneous judgments and there actually never was.

Q: It feels like a full stop...there's nothing more to know. The "you" you think you are and the "world" you think you live in are nothing more than thoughts arising. The rest is unknowable. So relax.

C: No one can "relax" yet that relaxing can happen once the nonconceptual seeps into the concepts and melts them all. But that is just another concept.

NO concept can ever come within a million miles of what IS. Then (NOW, there is ONLY NOW) life is as it ever was and shall be, a Dance of Being-Presence-Joyousness. For no one, AND the someone! What FUN it is to BE!

Follow-up

Q: Charlie, I am always amazed at how LOVE just cuts through the bullshit... leaving a glorious path of destruction and not one single thing to hold on to.

I am going to be brutally honest...I feel truly lost. Every single spiritual method I've tried has failed. I laugh because I can hear you (and Jeff Foster, to name another) rejoicing, "Ah, the lad (no one) has arrived at the gates of the Promised Land"). It doesn't feel that way...it feels completely dead...arid and stale. And, quite frankly, if I read or hear another spiritual teacher tell me, "you've already got it...it's staring you right in the face!" I might just vomit. I'm tired of books, tapes, lectures...the whole effing scene... it just seems to me to be self-indulgent nonsense ... spiritual masturbation.

So, I'm left with...THIS. I know that sounds really spiritual, but I assure you, it's not. I see "this" as a slow and grinding march to my inevitable death, all the while attempting to reconcile with a neurological disorder that has taken every identity I cherished: musician, artist, worker, husband...blah, blah, blah...I know it's a "poor me" story, but I can't seem to shake it.

So, when not occupied with other things, I spend my days trying to understand what so obviously cannot be understood. I create formulizations like the one I sent you...something to grab a hold of to make this meaningless existence more bearable (btw, I'm not suicidal even if I may sound like it. My brother once told me that life was a marathon and you had to finish the race...that made a deep impression on me). I listen to you, Jeff Foster, Scott Kiloby ... all lovely and loving people who have awakened (I know, nobody awakens ... I've given up on the Advaita-speak a long time ago...very onerous) and it's not words they're using but the place from which they are spoken. It is a place of peace and restfulness ... and love. I've basically given up the search. For me, there is nothing to find and I'm tired of looking. I know that can be interpreted as a very "spiritual" statement as well ... take it more as a "Bleep it, I give up" kind of thing.

C: You can't give up what you are not doing. It's being done! If YOU could give it up you would have done so a LONG damn time ago, yes? Giving up is impossible. That is the word: IMPOSSIBLE. 'Cuz YOU ain't doing it

What Is IS and what ain't ain't. But not for YOU. The gate to Paradise is forever closed to any "me" or "you".

You aren't in charge here! It's the utter innocence (in no sense) of the seeking and in the bottom pit of never ever 'finding,' in the empty horror of deep resignation (ah, bleep this!) and deep despair (too much, can't bear it!), and in the very heart of THAT, the Gift is found. Bad news: YOU cannot DO this, this seeing at and thru the Heart of what is arising and is resisted. Good news? YOU cannot PREVENT it. Better yet, just LOOK without thinking about this. "Seeing with naked Awareness".

In the absolute failure of the mind to get what it wants (peace, freedom, love etc) even after 30 or 40 years of practices, gurus, satsangs and all the other dogmatic spiritual bullshit, then in the frustration of failure to get there can be the opening to this as-it-is-ness. Hopeless Despair is a great seed of liberation!

You will NEVER get enough of what doesn't work. So long as there is a fixation on a false me-me-me, this me will appear as I WANT THEREFORE I AM.

And no matter how much you get IT IS NEVER ENOUGH. Like the James Bond movie title said, "The WORLD Is Not Enough".

That's the hardest thing for the seeker to hear! So the way this is happening over there is no mistake. It's Oneness inviting you Home.

No Concept Is What You Are

To say what you are in "words" is absolutely IMPOSSIBLE. No concept, no word, no phrase, no "pointer", no assertion, no declared "me", is actually real... it's all just words. No matter how lovely or ugly, words are words and that is ALL they are. Since what You are is NOT a word, how could a word "describe" that You, that Reality, that space? These words ain't gonna do it either.

The cage of concepts is just that ... a cage made of words about which fifty billion words are said, written, repeated, believed and turned into religions. It is all just plain old BS.

Yet That TOO is Not TWO...

Spiritual Practices End Up In Failure

The BAD NEWS is, if you are a spiritual seeker engaged in meditation, self-inquiry, chanting, guruseva, ascending, doing zazen, studying ancient texts, hangin' out in some satsang or other, YOU ARE DOOMED to FAIL. But only 100%! Now that also may be the GOOD NEWS ... IF the Message is heard. Not heard by YOU. You are an idea-in-mind with NO power or volition. But in Oneness, Timelessness, this radical Message may "sink in" ... Heart To Heart, so to say...

Clarity notices this: ALL "spiritual practice" is bound to end in absolute FAILURE. Why?

Because any "practice" assumes the existence of a person who is not whole and complete doing something to attain wholeness and completion. Plus the assumption of time, and "a someday" which simply NEVER EVER COMES. It's like that line from the Beckett play (paraphrasing) ... Waiting for Godot. It is HORRIBLE. Godot NEVER COMES. The cosmic joke is that all the while these assumptions are operating, allowing the survival of a cherished "seeking me", the One Subjectivity (call that Love, Being, Presence or whatever) shines ever fresh BEFORE the practice begins, while the practice is going, and after the practice stops, whispering softly I AM and that IS what you are seeking (but there is no-one whispering, this is just a way to point to what is actually always so.)

The caveat always is clarity, or understanding, has got NOTHING to do with The Timeless Absolute. Zero to do with Liberation. Nada. Zilch. Zip! Intellectual Clarity is the booby prize. So long as there is the idea-me and the conviction I AM, I really DO exist, I am ME, and the world is out there and NOT what I AM, then the shit will keep hitting the fan. And trying to get rid of seeking and trying to NOT practice is just another survival ploy the phantom I uses to survive.

If you are reading this and concluding, "Well hell, there is no hope. This message is so nihilistic. It's hopeless bullcrap" then there might be a glimmer of light poking through the dung heap of religious and spiritual dogma. Because it is hope that keeps you in apparent bondage. Yet this message is not really nihilism. In the dropping of that "story of me" and the evaporation of these false beliefs ... convictions! ... in "me", "time" and "someday", the absolute FULLNESS of All-Of-This is just ... stunningly gorgeous. (But for no one; that's the catch!)

But YOU cannot gain that. There is nothing that will work, NOTHING. Because there IS no you that was ever or ever could be apart from the Immensity of All That Is. So (not that you can 'do' this) ... Love thyself. As you is and as you ain't.

Period. Full Stop. So what's for lunch? Anything good on TV?

Where IS Control?

It seems that, from my experience, that in no place is the illusion of free will and control more dominant and powerful-appearing than in driving racing cars. You damn well better assume you have control, and the free choice, to commit to a turn at 160 MPH, to brake that little bit later, to pass where it looks like suicide etc, when you are driving one of those things.

Yet the evidence keeps coming up over and over ... you lose a wheel at 160 and you are outta control and crash; someone spins and sends you careening off the road outta control; it rains unexpectedly and you lose it in a puddle as your tires aquaplane and you are outta control; the engine eats itself for lunch while you are leading and you are outta the race, etc etc.

But us racers would ignore the message and keep right on assuming we have free will and are in charge.

Until it gets SO obvious you just can't ignore the fact that control is an illusion any longer.

That is when "your head goes into the tiger's mouth", as Sri Ramana Maharshi put it. Now you are asking the question "IS there any reliable and REAL control in this world, for me?" and the search for what is really going on begins.

Is Awareness 'The Absolute'?

Q: I have a question regarding what has been referred to as the "Absolute" or the Supreme State. Sri Nisargadatta Maharaj said that we are the changeless awareness that illumines the infinite content of consciousness.

C: I stand by that for sure!

Q: To me it is obvious that I am, and that there is this eternal, never-changing presence of awareness in the background - my question is regarding whether or not this awareness is actually what I am in the very deepest sense.

C: Yes, you are that Light of Awareness that shines forth as Consciousness (I AM).

Q: Although Maharaj and many others say that you are this awareness, he also mentions that you are the Absolute, which is "beyond awareness", beyond the sense of "I am", and that the absolute transcends birth, being, and death.

C: Here you kind of get hung up on the semantics or languaging of what IS and PRIOR to language and semantics. Using a word - "Awareness" - to point to The Absolute is just that – a pointer. Awareness is the objectless Subjectless Light of Being. Consciousness is the KNOWING "I am", there IS existence, consciousness, aliveness.

Q: It is also stated that beingness or "I am" is dependent upon the body-mind and disappears when the body dies.

C: Correct. The body-mind is like the candle and consciousness is like the flame that consumes the candle, whereupon as the last bit of fuel is exhausted the flame goes out. But the Light that IS cannot be extinguished because That is NOT an object. Call it a Flameless Light if you like. But bear in mind that no word can ever capture it because it is That which gives essence and appearance to the presence and the absence of the body-mind and consciousness.

Q: Is there a difference between the changeless in which everything, even the "I am", happens, and the Absolute?

C: Yes and no. The changeless is not an object that comes and goes and therefore IS The Absolute. Yet that Absolute appears AS everything, arising here and now in this timeless moment, so to speak...

Q: I guess what I'm getting at is whether or not I'm actually aware of the Absolute,

C: NO! You ARE the Absolute so to "be aware" of that you would have to be separated from that and there is no separation between you as consciousness (I AM) and The Absolute. These are, as is forever POINTED to, NOT Two. Or, "One without a second".

Q: Because I feel a strong need to abide fully in the state I was in before I was born and that is unaffected by death.

C: You already do abide as That. Trying to recover that seems to obscure that. Pause thought right now for a timeless instant: Here and now you ARE and already always abide AS that. You are just trying to capture it as if you were separated from that. That is a fool's errand!

Q: Is this simple, ever-present presence of awareness that I feel the Absolute, or is even this just a transient state that disappears sooner or later, and if so how does one realize the Absolute?

C: "One" does NOT "realize the absolute"! Who is there to do that? Where is any separate entity that is NOT already whole and complete, not already The Absolute? This is the ignorance of a mind that takes itself to be separate – yet that mind is just a notion, an idea of a person apart from The Absolute. Do a bit of looking for that so called person with a separate substantial existence apart from Being, Awareness, Aliveness itself and see what you find. I promise you will come up empty handed. And in that cognizing emptiness you are as you already always are will be have forever been – the Living Buddha-Nature, this Absolute arising as Being.

The bottom line is, YOU ARE THAT. Full Stop.

The Wisest Man In The World

Many years ago there appeared a wise peasant farmer who lived and farmed a plot of land in China.

He had a son who, though an idiot, was the gleam in his eyes - he certainly adored the boy as only a parent can. He also had one horse - a beautiful horse, which was not only his favorite and beloved possession, but also the workhorse for the farm.

One day the idiot son left the corral gate open and the horse escaped from his grounds and disappeared into the mountains outside the village.

The villagers came to him one by one and announced their condolences. They said, "You are such an unlucky man. It is such bad fortune."

The peasant answered, "Who knows. Maybe it's bad luck, maybe it's good fortune."

The neighbors shrugged and left.

The next day the horse returned, followed by twelve wild horses that followed him into the corral; the farmer noticed this, smiled, and securely locked the corral gate, warning his son, "Please dear boy, do NOT leave the gate unlocked again". The boy promised to do his best.

The same neighborly people returned and told our wise man about how lucky he was. "It's such great good fortune!"

The wise man replied once more, "Who knows. Maybe it's good fortune, maybe it is not. Who knows"?

As it happened, the next day his one and only son was attempting to break in one of the wild horses when the horse threw the boy and the boy broke his leg.

Once more everyone came to console him. They said, "It's so bad."

Again the farmer replied, ""Who knows. Maybe it's bad, maybe it's good."

Three days passed and his poor idiot son was limping around the village with his broken leg, when the emperor's army entered the village announcing that a war was starting and they conscripted all the young men of the village for a suicidal battle against overwhelming odds. However, they left the son since he had a broken leg.

Once more, everyone was so jealous of our wise man. They surrounded him talking about his good luck. "It is so good for you," they said. He answered all thus, ""Who knows. Maybe it's wonderful, maybe it's terrible. WHO KNOWS"?

And obviously - the story goes on - forever.

Who claims to know, knows NOT. – Ancient saying

Finding What Was Never Lost

Q: Hi Charlie, There was a recent shock in this mind-body organism as it was discovered that there is not the unborn and the born as two things.

C: Shocking indeed! But ... to whom?

Q: Is it true that the unborn is also consciousness at play?

C: Conceptually, sure. Consciousness at rest, Consciousness in motion, are NOT TWO. Consciousness or Beingness IS all there is.

But the concept is not the reality of This Nondual Isness. Now: What is That which asks and what is That which answers? BOTH are only appearances in what is Real -- YOU are That in which question and questioner appears. So in this, there is no "truth" -- and all there IS is "truth". Not Two

Q: It has been a pointer to see that there is an infinite context and then there is whatever is being experienced as the finite.

C: Finite and infinite are both this -- and neither is this. So – that is still linguistically just conceptual dualism. AKA bullshit, not to put too fine a point on it! You see, "Context" and "Content" are NOT Two. And in any case BOTH are merely concepts! This that is pointed to is that Understanding beyond concepts and THAT is the not-conceptual-natural-understanding that belongs to No One.

Q: What got knocked out was the perception that the unborn is emoting a play of form and function. This statement now seems separate. The unborn and the dream are "not-two."

C: So that IS cool! And, Not-Two, of course! But caution that the concept is NOT the actuality! So that is all okay so far as "language" goes, but THIS is prior to language -- it's sensed "here" that this is seen "there" by no-one, yes? But all this is just bubbles of Being - an appearance in (or as) what you are -- This Empty Presence. Yes?

In any event it does sound like there was/is a sense of this timelessness – I describe this as a "dying before you die" to paraphrase the sage Bankei. Yes? But again for whom? :-)

Q: It was in the context of reading some Ramesh [Balsekar]. There was also something said by him that spoke to that -- there is only pure functioning.

C: Yes. This is (as a pointer) the "functioning of Totality" but the concept is NOT what is pointed to by Ramesh, or this appearance, or any so called "other" in the guise of "teacher". Or "friend". By the way, utterly irrelevantly, "I" do adore the appearance called "Ramesh"!

Q: If this shift is one of truth then what else can be said about this?

C: Absolutely nothing. There is NO "truth" in THIS. Because "truth" is concept and THIS so-called "shift", which happens outside of time and to no-one, is Beyond Concept. That said; well … welcome to the Home you never left!

Mind you, this can be a very common "experience" and the warning here is do not take ANY "experience" to be the Reality of what is pointed to. This is beyond concept and beyond experience. What does that leave? Nothing. Just That. That, No Thing, yet appearing as Every apparent Thing -- THAT Thou Art!

So finally look into this, and ponder: "Francis Crick - Nobel Prize recipient in medicine for deciphering the DNA code said, 'You, your joys, sorrows, memories, ambitions, your sense of identity, free will and love are no more than behaviors of a vast assembly of nerve cells'." – And, "Anything that appears in the manifested reality - whether it appears as a thought, mind, body, other, no-one, – anything, nothing - is, in the final understanding, just appearance in a non-conceptual awareness". ~ John Greven

So: Where is the doer in this? There is NO shift, NO awakening, NO realization. NO "truth". All there is -- is all there is.

That. Only That.

Q: I have fully understood that I have always been the awareness behind the world, the world has never touched the real me.

C: This Infinity of Being (or Awareness, sometimes used as a synonym for Being) has never been absent. Try to escape Being! Cannot be done. The point is, this – Being – is BOTH Silence and Sound, Stillness and Movement, awareness and content OF awareness. Being is BOTH this empty background "behind the world" AND the appearing "world" of forms and time, locations and apparent persons, trees, cars, bombs, presidents and peasants. All there IS is One, Being everything. Note well that one word: Everything. In short the "real me" IS BOTH "the world" and the "awareness behind the world". Advaita: It points to This One-NOT-TWO-Ness of ALL of this! Nothing appearing as everything; one essence Being both no thing and every thing and all that arises as this "manifestation of essence" "between". Being nothing, wisdom; being everything, love. NOT two.

Q: However I go back and forth between feeling like the absolute and feeling my humanness instead of just being the witness of it.

C: That is just not true. And if you seek a "feeling of absoluteness" you will forever fail! "Absolute" and "Relative" are simply two apparent aspects (or linguistic labels devoid of any actual substance) of this One Ocean of Beingness! So seeking to get and hold onto that is a fool's errand. Who is separate to seek? Do you find a separate I-person apart from Being-Awareness-Aliveness??

You as Being don't move and change yet all that changes appears not only IN that timeless space but is also arising presently AS the "manifest aspect" OF that timeless space. It is NON duality – meaning, NOT two. Or, One-Without-A-Second. It cannot be attained. And, It cannot be lost!

Q: How do I stabilize as the ultimate witness?

C: "You" do not exist apart from totality, the One. Look for a separate "me" and you find only what is Real:

Nothing/Everything.

So where is any question of stabilizing? This idea of "witness" also assumes something to be witnessed by a witnesser and seems to favor the witness over the totality. That is pure dualistic nonsense. What assumes it is separate and a witness is only arising in words, language, and these sounds we call words cannot actually divide anything! Another way to see this is, if there is indeed ONLY ONE, then even these words and ideas and assumptions are ALSO that One. You simply cannot separate yourself from Everything. Who is it that assumes it is separate and asks this? Look and see if there really IS a "separate one" and then ask yourself, how can an assumed entity which is nothing but a temporal appearance of a thought either divide from totality OR stabilize as totality?

What we point out here is that EVERYTHING IS THAT. All there is, is Being. Being seemingly separated and being seemingly whole. Being all experiencing and all surmising and imagining and speculating and opining. There is ONLY Being and THAT is what is always so, eternally Real. In that there is no "me" and yet you are, knowing I AM.

Q: You have my deepest appreciation and respect, thanks for all your help.

C: Firstly, you are of course very welcome. But secondly: No one needs help to be this Totality of Being. All these ideas of helper and helpee are false assumptions of separate entities that on investigation simply cannot be found to exist apart from Being. All there is is Being and That is what is. Now paradoxically even these false assumptions are also Being, appearing as the seemingly separate subject and object. But do understand at the deepest level that nothing is actually separated and that language is simply telling itself lies! (Of course that "understanding" is a direct NON-conceptual knowingness that is already fully known and this belongs to NO ONE.) In summary: There is simply nothing to get – there is ONLY Being, being even this! There is no real "person", no "individual" anywhere anywhen. The undivided Whole cannot be split apart. Full Stop. regardless of how many assert that there is separation. Repeating a false assertion cannot ever make it true.

Assert the earth is flat. Does that make it true? NO.

Assert I am me and separated from others and this world. Does that make it true? NO!

Again, Full Stop.

Ponder this: "There is no deepening of what you are. Your nature is full and complete as is. All bondage and confusion is caused by concepts of being something other than you are and granting belief to those notions. Reality, or your fundamental identity, is not a matter or approach, time or development. That is the beauty of it. It is not becoming, but being what you are". (From John Wheeler).

And this: Timeless Loving Oneness Cannot Be Known. To "know" Oneness there would have to be a sense of separation FROM Oneness. Who cannot see the fault in that logic?

You may like to engage in a phone chat about this. *Details regarding that are on the consultations info in the back of this book.*

Follow-up

Q: (After a phone consultation) It occurred to "me" that I ....whoever .....I was, am dreaming up a Charlie, to wake up a "me", neither of which really exists separate from the whole of Beingness. If (says his name) has no free will neither does Charlie because in truth neither one exists! There is just THIS. The mind makes it far too complicated. When it is understood that nothing has any free will everything is accepted, because it is in truth one anyway, that does bring peace, there is nothing to do, plan or try to prevent its all just happening.

C: Excellent news! Now just "stay put". Love ya.

"There is no greater mystery than this: Being Reality ourselves, we seek to gain Reality". – Sri Ramana Maharshi

What IS 'The Final Understanding'?

Q: I hear about a "Final Understanding" and I wonder, can you say what that is?

C: There is only Being and Thou Art That. That is The Understanding that IS perfect peace, that "peace which passeth 'understanding' (mental knowledge)." (Note the capitol U).

Now: The more "useful" question is, who and what and where is that "I-me" that asks this, and considers or believes somehow that there is something other than this beingness-presencing here and now, for this me-thought to "attain someday"?

Where is that "me"? If you claim "I am me", well, is that really true? What's your evidence? In your own being-experience?

Notice that it is a self referral conception while the non-conceptual Is-Ness remains eternally untouchable and lovingly allowing it all to seem real – until the pointers come at that and an investigation happens. Then it's clear and obvious that you ARE and that is not a "me-identity". In short, it was a dream that no one woke from.

Here's The Good News:

There is absolutely no reality to, or need for, some imaginary "shift", "awakening", enlightenment" or any other conceptual-experiential story that the seeker tells herself or himself is not happening yet despite all his or her practices and inquiring etc. None. Why? Because in actual FACT you already ARE, and that Is-Ness is all that's being pointed to as your True Self, the Eternal Awareness behind the appearances and stories.

Or another way to point to it … The "shift" is one of perspective; OUT of the false assumption of being "me" and being apart from Totality. That is already always what IS so "shift" ain't a great pointer, but all of this descriptive expression is limited by the dualism of language. That is why we say don't look at the words, look where the words POINT. The words are only a map and not the territory; a signpost and nothing more. "The finger that points to the moon is not the moon."

Undeniably You ARE. The I AM is the one FACT you can count on. THAT is absolutely always so. You IS and you know you IS.

This Is-ness, this singularity called "I AM" is YOU, Being, being conscious OF being. (NOT the concept, but rather, the Nonconceptual Beingness, that is what I mean here.)

This pure open I AM is undeniable yet so often overlooked until it's clearly pointed out. There never really was "an energetic contraction" or a "flip-flop between 'me-ing and be-ing'" – all that stuff is an irrelevant and meaningless story, of a believed in and assumed believer story, told by words and what you are has never been a word! (If "you" are a word which one are you? If you are a word how come that word is not there all the time, even in deepest sleep?)

When it gets pointed out from clarity that no such entity as a me ever existed, that what you are arises from absolutely nowhere as the consciousness that is present and aware of being present, then the inauthentic assumption of a separate "me" fades quite naturally and effortlessly. There is no need for protracted practices or asking endlessly 'what am I?' (which is another mental story happening right within the Is-Ness that is Aware and Awake as conscious presence.) When clarity dawns through the story and what is seen is the un-doubtable light of being-presencing, then the search ends as the seeker is no longer a focus in mind. The mind is seen as words, feelings, emotions, story, and storyteller, appearing in the empty fullness of the luminous love that allows the whole show to appear and subside like a hologram appears as an "expression" of Laser Light.

Let's be really clear on this point: a still mind is still a mind. A peaceful state is still put a passing state. That state, that mind (thoughts including the core thought "I") all are appearing and disappearing in the whatever-word-you-like such as Beingness, Nothingness, Emptiness that You really Are.

This is what is pointed to by all pointers, such as "know thyself". What John Wheeler points to as "The Light Behind Consciousness". (A book I highly recommend, by the way.) The

True selfless nature of That is ... Love.

So ..... that's a lot of words to point to the wordless natural and original statelessness that you truly are. Perhaps something will be seen. However as we point out the obvious clear presence of consciousness, arising on the no thing of the Ultimate Absolute Nondual Is-Ness, if the clear seeing of timeless reality happens for you, then the words will have been worth typing.

What Is A Who?

Q: I am asking "who am I?" 24/7 as much as I can…

C: Okay: Now there is just one tiny question …

Who, or What, is asking 'who am I'?

All arises from out of no where - to whom? And who asks this? Love asks for itself to be known yet it is already here already now already forever for no-person everywhere now.

Ponder this from "Paradise Found" – Chapter 75:

> Question: Awareness of I AM seems to be the key that unlocks the door that isn't really there. Staying with the Awareness I AM seems to be so simple, pure and natural. But then along comes an identification with some event or aspect of "the story" and whoosh a trap door seems to open into the jungle of thought and confusion. No light in that jungle. A complete "forgetting." Round and round I go trying to see and sort it out (suffering) until finally I give up (Surrender). That Surrender seems to lead back into the light.

> C. Yes, and ALL of that happens in this Presence of Awareness. This Awareness is NOT a "thing" that comes and goes. IT IS. And this Isness registers all the comings and goings of thoughts, sensations, identifications with a story, feelings, sensations … sentience appears in That and THAT is what NEVER changes. You cannot escape That. IT IS, Being-Awareness-Aliveness, present and clear prior to and during and after all movements of thoughts feelings etc. Surrender? Who is there to do that? Dissolution of the false happens when there arises an investigation into the nature of the I or me we have mistakenly taken our self to be.

Q: How to stay in the Awareness of I AM and let the story flow?

C. You cannot escape that. Wanting to "stay in That" is happening IN that. It is like water to the fish: So clear and obvious that it is overlooked (but the analogy falls short because Awareness, unlike water, is NOT a thing you can grasp or know.) Awareness is the Silence of Stillness knowing; the knower and known are illusions arising IN that Being-Awake-And-Aware Aliveness that is the Real. THAT is non-conceptual and therefore cannot be grasped by the "I" which is itself only another concept. That I can never "know Oneness." You are NOT that I-thought which tries to stay with I AM. Being IS and that you are. Attempting to stay in That is a flip strategy for avoiding That.

This Puzzles Me...

Q: This puzzles me. Ramana Maharshi says you can't deny yourself because you are here, true enough but after you are not here [body dies] how are you to know the self or where is the self then.

C: Well, who is this asking the question? What is this "me" that is puzzled and where is it located? To paraphrase Zen – confusion (being "puzzled") and paradox are the guardians of the gateless gate to Paradise.

Sit with the dilemma, the paradox:

There is NO self and yet you ARE. But you believe you are a separate entity that has additionally identified itself as a body – believed to be "MY body". The conviction (mental belief) "I am the body" is the delusion of the false self center, the idea of I, I AM, I AM ME. And this ME IS this body that "I" seem to OWN.

All of that is based on that seeming solid belief, "I am ME", and all that is, is language, energy, formed into a seemingly solid "entity" -- yet the pointer is ALL of that is ASSUMED and NOT real on direct evidence.

That false self-center known in the mind as "me" dies into deep dreamless sleep, wakes into dream during sleep as a self-centered witness watching and identifying as a character in the sleep-dream, dies into the sleep dream into deep dreamless sleep, wakes after sleep and dream into this seeming persistent waking-state dream... what wakes up and takes itself to be that "me"?

There is no answer to the question who am I? Asking that to get an answer - and asking a clearly unanswerable question about "what happens" to "me" when that body dies?, is a futile quest! It will lead only to more and more frustration as the question only produces confusion. This is the ego's never-ending story of a false self with no substance or actual independent existence or power apart from the Whole of this play of Consciousness.

So let that confusion bubble and boil and perhaps the false self center will boil away leaving what already IS right here right now, timeless awareness, being itself with no alteration, unmodified, infinite, with no add-ons … just … I AM … Awake. Not "I am this or that". Just – I AM. Not the conceptual thought-feeling-sense but the Beingness POINTED to by the concept I, I Am. As the ancients said it, I Am That I Am. Period. Stop.

Where is a "body" with a name and a self concept, a self image, a personality (persona - mask!) - without words, ideas thoughts - i.e. language? You are the Truth, the Light, PRIOR to Consciousness, Prior to the assumptions that go "I am – I am me – I am the body so when body dies I die". So your question is coming out from a false paradigm, a false context, the assumptions "I am separate from Totality and this body is who I am".

So your question is coming out from a false paradigm, a false context, the assumptions "I am separate from Totality and this body is who I am".

Ponder on these things and write again if and when the Spirit moves you to.

With Love,

I Am That I Am.

The Seeker Is Addicted To I-I-I

Q: I have some issues with "practice" that I may need some advice on. Since embarking on the journey of 'self' abidingness if there is such a word, it has been both fun and challenging, tough when I let my attention slip and slack off about the practice thinking that's it, and I would fall back a little. The sense of oneness comes and goes, sometimes I would feel all fear has dissolve for days sometimes even weeks and than I would fall back into it again.

Prior to the last email I sent you, I was actually suffering from a dip or I would call it a dark night of the soul - depression, massive anxiety in social environments, etc. I felt totally alone purely and solely by myself. I felt nowhere to go to and no one to go to [for help] - especially having been a student of meditation and metaphysical studies I had come to realize I knew nothing, so it felt like a struggle to unite and be what I knew. It really felt like my world was falling apart, I wasn't happy at work and my relationships with friends were a total mess...and spiritually I am not doing well either You know it actually started about 3 years ago when I came to a halt in my theoretical / philosophical search.

During that time I only held one thing in mind, that I am not my body, mind, nor emotions - and the world is my projection -and held on to the I AM. I must say it wasn't easy.

But now my external situations and circumstance has improved and I can feel somewhat I am coming out from the dip, things are 'lighter' but there is one issue that I am still having some problem dealing with...can you help give some pointers...that is social anxiety!!!...although I had somewhat been much better in comparison to say last year - the anxiety attack is not that great, but at times it still gets the better of me - in fact I just experienced one this evening out meeting new people - the thing that gets to me is this, the whole day I would feel calm and than BANG - it hits me...it doesn't feel good because it depletes me and I feel less empowered after...it would take a lot more to get back into shape again later.

The question is this, what am I not seeing that is keeping this illusion going - and what can I do to accelerate my healing?

C: My friend, you have an addiction. A huge addiction. You are addicted to your sense of being separate, of "being a person apart from the Seamless Whole". You call this person-entity by the name "I". In this message you said "I" – I this I that I-I-I– ! No less than THIRTY times! You claim – in your prior message, and in this message - to have been looking into this. Your constant reinforcing of that "I" that you are addicted to as a being apart completely contradicts your assertions.

So the first thing to come to grips with is that YOU ARE AN ADDICT. Addicted to your false sense of separation. As with any addiction, there is the possibility of a cure through intervention. In this case the best intervention MIGHT be the time honored method taught by Sri Ramana Maharshi – the inquiry into the nature of the I, called Atma Vichara, or Self-Inquiry. This is one of a huge number of possibilities and ultimately there is no way to know if this or any other method of investigation will reduce and eliminate the false belief, the addiction to an I sense, a believed-in self-center, that selfish clod of complaints that is constantly self-referred and self-reinforced due to a lack of deep looking.

As Sri Ramana Maharshi said, "The thought 'who am I?' will destroy all other thoughts, and like the stick used for stirring the burning pyre, it will itself in the end get destroyed. Then, there will arise Self-realization."

The kicker is a big paradox: If there is no person in Reality, if the "I": is merely a powerless thought with no ability to fix or change anything, then WHO asks "Who Am I"? When it comes to that, a deeper insight may indeed follow. The suggestion is to try it. Drop the "self-abidingness" of focus on I AM and reverse course (since it clearly is NOT working!) and instead, ask that unanswerable question, and only that - WHO AM I? Refuse to entertain the addiction; exert the intervention.

Follow-up

Q: You peeled off my title: Advanced Spiritual Student, and a sense of nakedness went through the body as I read your email. I was wondered why there was a sense of fear lurking just prior to reading you email. Perhaps the trickster didn't want to 'see' itself....I am truly humbled. Who am I? Really for the first time, I can honestly say I Don't Know!!! What falsity who and what has been meditating and researching?? Ha ha Who is thinking I am getting it and not? What gets it and what fails??? It feels silly just thinking about it. WHO IS DOING THE PRACTICE!? I am doing this I am meditating I am practicing I I I the DOER is meditating - I AM PRACTICING I AM, then I am attached to the idea/feeling I am, but the one who is aware of the feeling of I AM is not the feeling itself??...as long as there is duality there is bondage? Is that right? I took the word "I am" for that which is - I thought I was following the instructions repeating I AM and trying to unite the mind and the feeling of it, but what I was really doing is dwelling on the IDEA but not the true reality of it - the EFFORT itself shows a dual mind, someone trying this and that. When I ask -Who am I, I do not know. [Am I] just this livingness?

C: There is ONLY Livingness, and Nothing. This that you are is Being arising as livingness.

But do NOT believe that. The Truth is Wordless, Timeless, locationless.

Finish it off. Get down under that mental stuff:

"The thought 'who am I?' will destroy all other thoughts, and like the stick used for stirring the burning pyre, it will itself in the end get destroyed. Then, there will arise Self-realization." - Sri Ramana

"Give up all questions except, 'Who Am I'?" - Sri Nisargadatta

Just do it. So long as there is a residual belief in an I apart from all, put that I to work and do this. Do it until the mind gives up the ghost and The Self that you Are is shining in plain view. Don't settle for the menu, the concepts: get the MEAL, the Oneness That you Are.

The Fictional Identity "I Am This Body" Is Suffering

When the identity goes onto flesh and bone, blood and guts, thought and feeling machinery called "This Body" that that identity as a born and sure to die body as I Am brings attachment or aversion. But only always.

When awareness "contracts" and appears or arises as consciousness the game is on!

Consciousness I AM, I EXIST (not the concept I but the pure I of empty consciousness or witnessing Presence) APPEARS AS empty and meaningless energy; that energy contracts and then that consciousness attaches to the brain-body apparatus, and from there on out there is always a sense of suffering, of something lost, of pain or pleasure. The identity now seems solid and the bones and flesh seem separated from Awareness and separated from Consciousness ... and then appear solid and really separated from the Life Itself ... as the positive-negative poles of the conscious identity called "I am this body, brain, thinking-feeling machine" contract more and more as life in the body goes on from birth to inevitable death. This identity is a vast cauldron of suffering as there is either attachment to the body (trying to extend its life) or aversion (really being so sick and tired of being sick and tired the consciousness just wants that body to die now as it has become a burden that can hardly be borne any longer.)

This identity, though false, is so seemingly real to all but a few called sages that the world population is largely doomed to suffering this illusion of birth and death.

What to do?

First off understand that you are Awareness, and that Awareness is PRIOR to the Consciousness of Being. Then understand that whether the body lives or dies is irrelevant to Awareness and even to Consciousness. And understand that Awareness and Consciousness while appearing as distinct are not actually separate, in the same way that a wave is not the ocean yet it is made of the same essence of water that the ocean is... and so the wave called Consciousness is both separate from and is essence the same as the ocean called Awareness.

What good is this conceptual knowledge to the suffering identified one who considers himself or herself to be this temporary apparently born and sure to die body? No one knows. But this understanding MAY bring a deeper insight into what is Eternal and Real distinct from what only SEEMS real (no matter how convincingly).

Most suffer and die in this identity. Few recognize another bigger possibility ... the Eternal Possibility of freedom, power and love... the freedom of Being. The power of Consciousness-Energy and the Love of what IS as it is.

Being lived by Awareness-Consciousness and no longer taking oneself to be a separate born-sure-to-die body brain apparatus is the Eternal Possibility of Being Itself.

You are already always free in This Presence, beyond body, brain, mind, emotion; This is the Understanding beyond comprehension and beyond seeking. Paradise Found.

You Are The One Unborn Self

Q: I caught one of your videos on YouTube and wanted to ask you if you have become broad enough to realize God, I call it God, you can call it what you like, out of existence and both in and out?

C: This Loving Oneness (God or whatever label you like) cannot Be Known. To "know" Oneness there would have to be a sense of separation FROM Oneness. Who cannot see the fault in that logic? Being, Awareness, Livingness is right here. That registers all thoughts, emotions, stories, identities etc. in Timeless Space. YOU ARE THAT.

Q: Yes, I do perceive this, what I was referring to was the process. Some would say that enlightenment is "now" and that it takes no time, and it does not, for those who are enlightened, but enlightenment does take time and it is a process when you are in the midst of it, at least it was for me, but I can only speak of my own experiences, not for yours or others. To realize God, is to realize God in existence and out of existence, and in both and be able to have sufficient ground, to be big enough to realize God both within and without as the one. To see God in gods terrible, torridness, and to see God's magnificent beauty and to have realized that underneath it all, its nothing, nothing to speak of.

C: Well said.

Q: You are Guru, I bow at your lotus feet.

C: YOU are "The Guru", there is ONLY You. NOT TWO. Don't bow to "my" feet, bow to The One, The Self that YOU are.

It's all the Mirror - The One Self.

Follow-up

Q: Ah, well Charlie, there is only one Guru in existence and that is "I". That "I" that is reading these words and that "I" that is typing them now, is Guru. "I", who am Guru acknowledge the Guru, "I" within you. Guru appears outside of you to push your awareness inward so that Guru within you may arise, that is the way I perceive it.

147

But I am preaching to the choir now, aren't I?

C: You always are what you are … Unborn

Q: I have climbed the mountain of myself. In this place, where the air is so thin, and the coldness of truth for most would be unbearable, I can look down and see where I have come from, and survey my surroundings. In this place where there are so few, I can see others who have climbed to their peak, summit or pinnacle, out there I can see you my friend, and I know that indeed I am in resplendent company.

C: You are NOT special nor am I. Because you are the mirror and I am the mirror – NOT Two. "We" remain as we are, Unborn, One I called We, one humanity called Us, one Self called ALL-THERE-IS.... and yet - there IS no IS... No guru no disciple no path no goal no space no time no self no other yet this IS that is NOT seems so very seems that it IS.

One essence... No Thing … appearing as .... Everything.

There cannot be TWO "No Things"! There is no individuals, no separate persons out there. You see your Self in the mirror of the empty mind, dear One.

This is just spontaneous … poetry. I have no Truth to tell or know, not here not now.

The One is all there is.

Chasing My Tail, Catching Nothing

Q: I have been trying to catch my tail hoping to find diamonds, jewels galore; I keep on hearing your "Stop, stop", hopefully someday I will.

C: So stop looking and notice

Are you aware?

Are you present?

Any doubt that you ARE, right here right now?

That "awareness of being" or "sense of presence" is the naked, natural state, we overlooked it but now it's time to come back to that home we never actually left. Just NOW. You are this NOW. That's it, over and done.

Q: Thanks for everything Charlie, thank you. After your last above note, in the night around 11 PM when the normal "I" that "I know" was pinned down with absolute attention, and an inquiry was made "Who am I?" for an unknown amount of time, everything vanished except the Love.

I AM, the normal I-self, the "me" I knew as I, was not there anymore. There was only a Love that cannot be described! There was I, I, I, I ... only. At 3: 00 AM that night a note was written to Charlie Hayes in love and thankfulness; there were no fingers to type no tabs to type on everything was I, and This I IS Love.

C: Nice! You actually wrote a note from One to One; Self to Self!

Q: Since then everything is peace and freshness; all unnecessary things that was a part of my life is gone-gone down the drain. That included art ventures, spiritual books, incense, rudraksha mala, mantras, Baba of Ganeshpuri, dried flowers, Baba's autographed books ... they all have no meaning anymore.

C: And none of it ever DID have any "meaning". Good "seeing" happening there.

Q: Now, about three weeks later, the inquiry Who Am I? goes on continuously. Occasionally the fear of the appearance cheating mind comes in with all its goriness the so called sweet addictions, and they do not find safe haven any more, too long. Still am afraid that the mind is sneaking in as I am communicating with you now and am mortally afraid to talk to you one to one on a telephone that opportunity you have offered so gracefully.

C: All sounds basically fine! "The mind" ... what is that? Where is any "mind"? Fear is a residue of a "me" trying to re-assert itself to avoid its demolition (the thought "Who Am I?" is the great compassion that destroys the ignorance of false assumptions).

If any trace of suffering remains root out the cause. This inquiry, when finished, leaves No Thing. And that No Thing is also Everything. THAT, we can call ... LOVE.

Now you know.

From Something To Nothing To Everything

After The Inquiry: There's No Seeking, No Seeker – Just The Ease Of Effortless Living... This dialogue took place over a five month period. The finishing of seeking brings profound peace and ease in daily life, as this "former seeker" demonstrates:

Q: There was a pointer I read somewhere a while ago that said "How am I aware or even know that I exist"? Now the so called problem that is arising in this awareness is a conflict that sounds different from your pointers (in the book "Perfect Peace"), which starts asking us first if we exist (yes) and if we are aware (yes) and to look at that. But although there was seeing for a moment into this and that it cannot be denied I don't understand why you hint us towards starting with the undeniable premise that we exist but the other pointer is putting our very existence into question and it is a good question how am I aware or even know that I exist?

C: Right. But keep in mind all these words are ONLY pointers! Don't get caught up trying to find a "right" pointer. ALL the pointers ONLY POINT and often there can be two apparently opposing concepts yet BOTH can point to the Timeless Spaceless IS that you truly are. Stop trying to figure this out! It cannot be understood; the answer is NOT in the mind. You ARE – LIFE IS – THAT is the answer the mind cannot hold. Because the mind (sounds, words, concepts, feelings, knowledge) appear IN that Space of Awareness that is lit by The Light of Beingness that you really really ARE!

This is UN-Figure-Outable! As John Wheeler says, "The pointers are only a reminder that you are not what you think you are. Before you think, you are. And that is perfect from the start".

Q: So my problem is that the pointer used in your other book, "Paradise Found", does "reveal" THAT. but I don't see why I accepted I exist so easily. I mean I think I exist.

C: THAT is the delusion, the ignorance that says "I think therefore I am". First you ARE, and then the thoughts arise.

Descartes had it Bass Ackwards! Drop that false concept now and SEE what IS is that YOU ARE but THAT YOU ARE is NOT a thought!

Q: Or better I am aware of a presence here that I cannot deny; but why is the first pointer second-guessing something that you or myself say is undeniable? I thought all pointers are pointing at THAT same thing that cannot be spoken about but is that pointer simply starting from another angle; there are 10,000 ways to God, as has been said. I think that some pointers start with showing you first what you are and I you finally see it for your-SELF. And then others start by showing you what you are not so that you can arrive at what you are.

C: This is a very good question. Yet there can be no answer that will be "TRUE". The Truth cannot be put into words because words are tools of distinction or division. This is why Lao Tzu said right out of the gate in the Tao Te Ching, "The Tao (BEINGNESS) that can be told is NOT the Eternal Tao". Moreover, you NEVER "arrive at what you are". You are ALREADY THAT and to try to arrive is the direct DENIAL of your True Nature. That is a spectacular ignorance, a spiritual crap idea that reinforces a false sense of being a separate, discrete entity. In the mind of mankind there seems to be a "veil" that separates a "me" from "everything else". But look for that veil, that ACTUAL separation and you find nothing! That - No Thing - IS your true nature. Spacelike, ordinary, being-aware. Just THAT and nothing else.

Lao Tzu pointed beautifully with his Tao Te Ching. The entire first verse says it all succinctly. Ponder it:

The Tao (BEINGNESS) that can be told is NOT the Eternal Tao.

The name that can be named is not the eternal name.

The nameless is the beginning of heaven and Earth.

The named is the mother of the ten thousand things.

Ever desireless, one can see the mystery.

Ever desiring, one sees the manifestations.

These two spring from the same source but differ in name; this appears as darkness.

Darkness within darkness.

The gate to all mystery.

Mystery equals NOT KNOWING. In Not Knowing there is Absolute Freedom, BEYOND or PRIOR TO both Being and Non-Being.....

Q: I just don't know what the first pointer is starting with, must be a really good pointer then?

C: Again, there are NO "right" or "good" or "wrong" or "bad" pointers! These concepts ONLY point to That which IS and PRIOR to concepts, PRIOR to experiences. Prior to "subject/object" is YOU, The Ultimate One Subject, The Absolute a Priori IsNess.

I AM THAT. YOU ARE THAT. There Is ONLY THAT. THAT is absolutely empty and absolutely full, utterly no thing AND every thing – the screen and the show, the witness and the witnessed, all is One.

Language seems to divide nothing and everything into two and many and gazillions of separate objects - but the impossible to understand PARADOX is that Both Are One, or Neither Are One, and All of This Is One.

If you had any control in this space I would say let the mind blow apart in Not-Knowing. But there is NO ONE in Charge Here! Or There. Or Anywhere. All there is, is all there is. This IS IT. There is nothing to get. Nothing! Nada! Zilch! Zip!

So: This Presence of Awareness IS and IS NOT all at once in Timeless Being, AS Timeless Being. Pause now and drop all concepts and notice that before there is any "thing" YOU ARE.

No kidding, that is IT. YOU ARE and YET You Are Not. Both Not Two. You cannot get this; you ARE this! And This is Love in action. Oneness Being Itself. Home.

Q: There seems to be amazing content and pointers in the audios you've sent. But I've come to the conclusion (yes inquiry is going on about who came to the conclusion, but besides that point...) I've come to the conclusion that although non-duality/Advaita is expressed beautifully by, John Wheeler, 'Sailor' Bob Adamson, Sri Nisargadatta Maharaj, Ramana Maharishi etc that they're just pointers and that I am being kept in the loop by listening to these 'talks' on that that cannot be spoken about.

C: Come back to that final unanswerable question: Who am I? There is NO "conclusion" to come to! Don't take your stand in intellect. Take you stand in No Thing. You are That: Space-Like-Awareness.

Q: So I wondered if you were aware that maybe these talks keep people coming back to search for more videos by you or wait for more audios to be sent.

C: If that is what happens. A memory here says that this happened for me during my back-and-forth dialogues with John Wheeler, Tony Parsons, Bob Adamson and others. There is NO control over that here and none for any seeking "them" or expressing "teacher" either. Who controls? No answer. That is the "final answer"! Ultimately all is One so there is NO answer to any question that will mean anything or be in any way significant.

Q: So I will take the pointer that you have given me and stay with that beyond all else.

C: Well, my friend, I suppose we'll have to see if that is what happens!

Q: Just one thing that isn't understood: The question is arising that if Advaita, or Reality, is beyond words why is it taught or pointed to?

C: "Advaita" means NOT TWO. So this Reality is both beyond and WITHIN all that IS and all that APPEARS. No separation exists anywhere – yet the sense-feeling "I am me and not you" persists until deeper investigation arises. This is Oneness seeking Itself! Totally bizarre in a profound way, yet so it seems to be that the One has divided itself and is now seeking to undivided itself. The cosmic Play!

The sun burns. The earth rotates. The galaxies shine. The pointing happens. ALL happens spontaneously all by itself. To whom? To No One which is also One and All. By whom? No one and yet the Life Force urges and out come words and music of The One. Like a cosmic Broadway Musical! Stunning, isn't it? The wonder of Being This?

Q: Who is trying to enlighten/teach people, who is trying to be saved by teachings?

C: Very good question – for you to ask YOU!

The question who am I (or what am I) has as it's "purpose" to stop that loop in its tracks. It's about the rediscovery that there is no person and yet Being Is. To paraphrase what Ramana Maharshi said, the thought 'who am I' will destroy all other thoughts and in the end will itself be destroyed, and there will arise Self Realization. The paradox is that the Self is already realized (you ARE and the knowing that you are IS The Self, empty, vacant, yet filled with the totality of all Universes, Galaxies etc and 'your' body/mind/spirit). Some say that this is Nothing Being Everything. So in FACT (NOT speculation or imagination or memory but in FACT) YOU ARE. This Is-ness that is ever new and contains all is the true nature of what is real. Then if confusion or doubt remains the question 'who am I' can be taken up to facilitate 'looking in to self' to see if a separate self-entity with any independent power apart from Totality can IN FACT be found!

Ponder this: "Your innate being stands forever outside of the domain of concepts. Call that the still, unchanging point. In fact, it is not even really 'still' because stillness and motion are attributes of appearances in consciousness. What you are stands beyond, or free of, all characteristics. Still, some pointer is used to get us to notice who we are. But even the pointers are dropped ultimately. What you are is not a pointer! The only thing that can make us suffer is the mind's concepts about how we are incomplete, defective or limited. It is not that we have to make them go away, because that is another concept! And also we are not creating them anyhow. But we can see them for what they are. In doing so, the belief and interest drops out of the limiting, self-oriented thoughts in the mind — and with it, the suffering and doubts". - John Wheeler

Q: I don't know anything anymore and although there is a feeling of regret that I'm letting go of a beautiful man by the name charlie go, the thought arises that if there is oneness than I can never lose you.

C: Who do you believe I am? Someone special and apart from you? Shoot that down. Blow up that pedestal. All Is One. I am you and you are me; One Presence, One Awareness, One Being.

Q: So I guess with ruthless compassion "let me be". Thank you and so long (sadness and feeling of loss). I love you my friend.

C: I love you back! Now, who is leaving whom? Understand this: That sadness and sense of loss arises as the ego's survival mechanism – when the existence of this ego, or "mistaken identity", is called into question, the reaction is often a sense of loss or despair. And a feeling of hopelessness may arise, or a sense of frustration, anger or any other moving of The Absolute as an energy of a language-emotion play. Let that be and look deep into it. Abandon hope in favor of rigorous looking! Who is angry, frustrated, resigned, or sad? And without those labels what is there IN FACT? Energy. That Energy is the timeless loving Universal Life Force. Let This Force ERASE you.

Who says Charlie is NOT exactly THE SAME as YOU? That is a flat LIE! A totally false belief, a phony assumption. Got it? The answer is dead simple. NOTHING is excluded from NON duality. ALL is ONE. Expression happens as the sun rises. All naturally effortless.

There is NO we, and yet, We are One. Ponder this, chew on this; gnaw this bone of contention until it crumbles and the false self drops into the Great Mystery. When you said "I don't know anything any more" you are touching your own final truth! Stay with that as best you can and keep looking with "who am I?" until there is no question or doubt left. The gift of effortless living and true timeless peace is at hand. Grab it!

Q: I am seeing changes ... there is not a caring anymore for people's approval which feels very empowering. The problem/question arose when a thought of superiority came about. It was seen and inquired about but the urge remained to showoff this feeling of having no limiting beliefs. So after thinking that no one cares how I feel or think a fear arose also that although I am feeling-understanding/resonating with the truth that apparently there are others out there who still think they are separate. And since it looks like 95% of people believe in separation then the whole world is a very dangerous place where everyone is looking out for number one. Wait, maybe this shows me that since I think that people think that they are still separate that I still believe deep down that I am separate? I am just standing out here in the wind with no clothes, no center and no reference point and it's scary. What makes it more frightening is that it feels as if everyone else has concepts that can help them or that they can cling to however false it be but I have no where to go no where to lean on and that anyone can take advantage of me since I have let go many defenses. But who has let go of these defenses? It keeps being found that there is nothing being found upon investigation! But it does not stop there seems to be a habit of wanting to be in control or thinking that there still is something separate. But who says this? I don't know, don't know. It's stupid because I heard the talks and I was nodding my head saying what else is there that can be asked but this load OF questions keep happening... Or am I just beating around the bush and I should keep with the question 'Who Am I'?"

C: YES.

Q: I'm just afraid that if there's no me who would want the women and good feelings. But I want them, can I keep them?

C: WHO?

There is nothing wrong with thoughts; it is only that you consider them to be about a "me" that doesn't have any substance; it's just thoughts, memory, imagination.

Look at it this way:

Here and Now You Are and That is ever-present, prior to, during, and after, all relative "states" of waking, dream, deep sleep, and regardless of how the brain erupts into thoughts and feelings, That natural, or eternal, state is being always, and forever remains endless and beginningless, absolutely untouched and unsullied by any appearance, and effortlessly serenely free.

Q: Very helpful; thank you so much. I see that absolutely no question is the right one because they are all part of consciousness which is reflected in the mind and I am not the mind which includes the thought that says I am not the mind. the only true fact is I am that I am. I of myself do not know nor do 'I' think "I'll" ever know it but who cares! Ha-ha!

C: Okay, good on ya!

Q: (Later) - My new question is this, 'I" wanted to go to Medical School but I see that the "I" might just be a set of assumptions and very strong belief systems. I guess I mean that I'm afraid that; what I set out to do and the motivating force that gives meaning and direction to my life, feels like it is being threatened and asking in essence do you really want to do this? I know the 'I" that is assuming all this is also part of consciousness and my maybe an aspect of the ego but I keep becoming fearful of letting go of control.

C: This entirely overlooks the fact that before any thought or question arises, you are, silent and aware. You mistake a thought - "I" - to be what you are. That is the ONLY issue to resolve: Who ARE you REALLY? Where is any real separate "I"? Who wants? Who asks this? Who are you? WHO!? That is what you stubbornly refuse to look at. Read the attached copy of "Paradise Found" three times before you ask another question.

REALLY!

(After a while, this arrived):

Q: I've really been feeling more freedom and less pull from habitual desires and have been smiling more so something clicked from our last discussion so that's the good news. But I have a question about this not-doing. It seems like this is a pathway of negation I read about some time ago; basically you negate everything that cannot be you (thoughts, feelings, emotions, mind, body, etc..) which would lead 'you' directly and nonverbally to the ever present Reality. Thing is that many take the void (nothingness) as the ultimate state and that that should also be seen to be an illusion and not accepted if it is void of love. Actually I don't actually merely verbalize "How am I aware or even know that I exist?" anymore because I know that was just pointers and there is no actual answer. So what I'm wondering........I don't know who cares forget it its just more analyzing ughh... at least 'I' am becoming aware of the vicious circle now but question is who is becoming aware? Charlie the problem is I'm losing ... I don't know ... I don't know .... wow I see how the search for enlightenment was being treated the same way as the attainment of any other 'thing'...I don't know. thanks again for the talks it was very humbling... wait ... if "I" am not interested/care/see the world as it is and see things as they are who will take care of me? I don't see how one can survive without an ego.

C: Ponder deeply what has already been shared. Read "Paradise Found" again. Give this more of a chance to "sink in". Challenging the assumption that your brain claims, namely, "I am me", get to the bottom of it all and see that this "me" is a GHOST. Take some time. Investigate. Then, feel free to write again if there is still any question.

Some time passes, then this comes, after a phone consultation:
Q: It is a blessing to have talked with you thank you so much.

C: My Pleasure.

Stay put in I AM, and BE what you are. Don't deny your essence of being ... No Thing.

And don't pretend to be what you are not ... an individual persona, masking the Infinity that You ARE.

I Love You.

You Don't "Have" This; You Are This

This one bears repeating: Q: For many years, my background was in Christianity, but for the last few years I have been steeped in non-duality...reading books, listening to audio downloads, watching videos. I realize that my true nature is awareness and that my old identity just doesn't exist.

C. You do NOT "have" a True nature. You ARE "True-Nature. Being, Just That.

Maybe you still seem to think you are a separate entity that owns something called a True nature. That is a common pitfall in these so called "teachings" and is very misleading.

Q: What has been bothering me lately is what is it that survives death? I realize that my true nature (awareness) survives of course, but is that it? Do we recognize ourselves at all after death? Or do we just fall asleep, have a good dream, and never wake up?

Just who is this that would die or be born, survive or not, dream or not? WHO? There is no reality to the assumed identity, EVEN an assumed identity called "I am Awareness". Or "I am everything" or "I am all there is". ALL identities are false, clouds of energy assuming a solidity that just ain't there in FACT...It's all a dream, all a mirage, a lake with no water. The Universe-Appearance is just NO thing LOOKING like everything! Like the mirage lake in the desert LOOKS like water but on closer looking is seen to be absolutely NOTHING.

Q: I sure would appreciate some clarity about this, and I was hoping you could help me out some. I've read all your books, but I just don't find much information that solves my question.

C. Okay, to directly answer the question the way you framed it, in the context in which it is asked:

NOTHING SURVIVES DEATH.

NO THING HAS ETERNAL EXISTENCE! ONLY No Thing!

That means, NO THING.

And YOU ARE that … No Thing.

So, the answer IS pointed to, in the books … notice what is repeated over and over. Always the mind is challenged to investigate its assumed identity as a "thing" with a solid separate existence. It is the answer the mind gets when the question is asked, "WHO asks the question?" Looking at that right now, what "answerer" is there? There is no answer, no one to answer, no thing at all, just emptiness, spacelike, yet awake and aware as Being-Consciousness-Livingness Itself … and what IS is The Eternal Nothingness PRIOR to "Consciousness." And you will NEVER "know" This ... The Eternal No Thing ... because you ARE This Eternal No Thing (appearing as every thing, as ALL is ONE Essence of Being; Not-A-Something yet Everything. IMPOSSIBLE to grasp. Give that up! Trying to grasp the essence is a loser's game, my friend.

The answer is NOT in or for the mind!

So: There absolutely is NO answer; there IS no "you" that was born and can therefore die. And that IS the answer. All that is born is a false idea of an "I" apart from everything/nothing. That is born and dies. Moment by moment.

As the questioner is always brought back to look, WHO asks this? WHO wants to know? WHO is concerned with this question?

Find that there IS no answer and the question dissolves along with the questioner. And liberation happens, but not for "you". This is liberation from "you" and not for "you".

All there is, is already liberation, already freedom. And so long as there is that veil of assumption, this liberation is forever denied to you. As long as you look for freedom that very freedom that IS remains forever beyond your grasp. But if the frustration with failing to find what you seek becomes potent enough, then there may be a fading of the seeker and a seeing directly for no one that there is nothing to attain, nothing to find, because there never was a "person' who was NOT free. If that happens, then we might call that … Grace.

But no one can make Grace happen!

The bottom line is Nothing Survives Death. And you are THAT ... No THING.

And That is Compassion, and Love, my friend. So BE as you are ... No Thing appearing as Every thing. And that is all there is for no one to get!

Follow-up:

Q: Wow! Thanks so much. That question was answered so completely and it is very much appreciated. Your answer will take a few readings, but it sure cleared up things nicely. Love and appreciation, and P.S. Thanks for not holding back!

C. You are very welcome, my friend. Stay in touch as and when The One moves that to happen!!

The Unseen Reality Which We Are

Q: What if... there is no rhyme or reason, it's all random! Potential for everything yes, but that which appears or happens occurs because there is energy for it, rather like bubbles popping on the surface of a pan of boiling water. No one knows when or where another bubble is going to occur only that there is the potential for it to happen.

The ego however seems to need to find reasons for every happening as the notion of random chaotic acts of energy appearing/disappearing within the space is too much for it to accept. Somehow even if understanding fails, the person (if one is believed to exist) takes comfort in thinking that at least God knows what's going on and maybe some day they might too. Comfort and control being the root causes.

Yet the truth seems to be, all that appears just does as energetic bubbling on the surface of awareness. A minute layer of seen-ness on the surface of the unseen reality which we are.

As quantum science has energy popping back and forth even appearing to be in two places at the same time, it's an illusion therefore to think that this dreamlike state makes sense.

It's all just happening here and now for no one by no one; it is, just it and we are that!

This moment exists literally just now, and it's the mind that tries to cello tape one minute to the next one and so create the illusion of time. That creates the illusion of action and consequence. Yet every single moment is 100% brand new, once only, never to occur again that way.

There is no purpose, there is no reason; it just is. Strangely enough that's so freeing, everything is allowed to come and go without commentary... awesome.

Many thanks, Charlie.

C: Great expression, clear as the light behind the sky!

I would not add anything to this. Not even Nothing!

Well maybe, just this:

You said, "it is, just it and we are that!"

There is no WE. There is ONLY That! :-)

Timeless Space-Light giving rise to nondual appearances of nothing happening to appear and these are Not Two...

Much Love,

Charlie

Q: Yes, absolutely!

C: Great!

"Identity" Is A MYTH

Q: I listened to a reading of [the late] Ramesh Balsekar's words recently. It seems that Ramesh was saying that there are two aspects to identity. There is identifying with the body which doesn't cause suffering and then there is identifying as the body and believing that this body is the source or initiator of the actions that happen through it. The belief in being an initiator or sourcer (if that is a word) is what brings about suffering.

C: I disagree. There are not "two aspects of identity". There IS NO IDENTITY in Reality – none whatsoever. The assumed identification as a thought-sense "I am me" is the core of suffering, NOT believing that a body is the source of its actions. What we try to point out is that the core of ALL so-called identity – whether there be identification with "body", "mind", "spirit", etc or any other concept - can only arise IF there is a fundamental wrong assumption of a core entity that stands apart from the whole. This is pointed to as the assumption that there is an "I" identity that could then be further identified as any thing at all! But is an assumption TRUE? Where's your proof that "you" are a thought - or any "thing" - apart from awareness? Moreover, while you assert a belief that "identifying with the body doesn't cause suffering", isn't it utterly obvious that identifying as that changing and gradually dying body form is bound to produce suffering? Isn't it clear that when you think of yourself as a "dying thing", you would naturally be afraid? Because it IS absolutely true that the body WILL expire sooner or later!

Q: It seems that there will still be suffering even without the belief in being an initiator.

C: As pointed out above, it is the false belief that the "I" thought is what you are that is the root of suffering.

Q: For example this body (me) ....

C: And THERE IT IS – the core assumption of a me and then the add-on of "me as a body". But without the presence of the simple awareness that is always here now, before any notion of "me" plus the added notion of "me as a body", these ideas could not even appear. Awareness is the necessary foundation for it all and that awareness is what you really are.

Look: where exactly IS this "me"? What is "it" made of? Does it actually exist as a substantial object at all? "Me" is a thought. "Body" is a thought. What is that IN which these thoughts appear and fade? That is NOT a thought, NOT any thing at all, yet, IT IS. That is the Real You.

Nonconceptual prior-to-language Is-Ness.

Now, when the identity (the notion of a "me" apart from The All) appears and is misconstrued to be the self, and then extends itself onto the ever changing physical apparatus, the suffering ensues.

There is just this one error of mistaken identity to correct: This is really good news! There is no need to deal with the array that radiates off the core misconception of what we are: just go right to the heart of the matter and deal with the core, the fundamental mistake, and the whole house of cards collapses.

Q: .... (this me) has an aversion to getting fat or the thought of getting fat. It also has an aversion to the thought of exercise and an attraction to the thought of eating sweets at times. It's seen that the aversion and attraction to various things is out of control. That still doesn't make it any less painful when they conflict. That seems like suffering.

C: Clearly that is a product of taking yourself to be a body, and a mind, a "me", that cherishes preferences! In addition, if you really knew beyond doubt that all that happens is happening out of anyone's control there would be no suffering. The suffering comes as the thought of "me" resists and makes efforts (which are thoughts resisting other thoughts) to exert control but there is NO possibility of really controlling anything with thought. Perhaps, you, as an assumed entity, just assume that you don't have enough "self-control", rather than recognizing that there is NO "control center" in you anywhere.

As is always pointed out here, all suffering happens from this single apparent cause, which is believing you are any thing at all, and seeing that this structure of conceptual thought arises due to the fundamental error; in other words, 1) Not knowing what you truly are, "namely" the Empty Fullness of Awareness Prior - To-Consciousness - Wakefullness, and 2) taking yourself to be a thing called "me" when what you are is not a thing, not a concept, not a perception and not a person separate from this clear awareness – your undeniable being which never changes and which you absolutely cannot deny.

Q: Nisargadatta says that I'm not this body at all - that what I am is this awareness of everything which isn't separate from anything.

C: Full stop!

And I must repeat, isn't it obvious that identifying as that changing and gradually dying body form is bound to produce suffering? This is so clear, that when you think of yourself as a dying thing you would naturally be afraid as it is absolutely true that the body WILL expire.

Q: The body is just one of the objects that arise in this subjectivity. At least that seems to be what he's saying.

C: "The body" is a CONCEPT arising in what you are. In essence "the body" is the Light of Being-Awareness, arising as energy patterning and appearing; it only looks solid, but in fact it's all just energy appearing as a pattern of light, the light of pure awareness prior to concepts; much like a hologram appears as a multidimensional object only because there is the Laser light seeming to cause it's appearance, but isn't it clear that the holographic pattern is actually MADE UP of that Laser light? It's the same with the entire manifest appearance. All there is is awareness-being-loving appearing as Nothing/Everything. That cannot be grasped – the answer is NOT in the mind - as is always pointed out. How could thought grasp non-thought?

Q: So does identity with an object (in this case this body) create suffering after all? Or maybe it's mistaking subjectivity to be one of the objects (this body). If I am this body then I am suffering.

C: Again it is the sense of being a separate "me" that gives rise to suffering. Start from the basic fact that you ARE, and that you are always aware that you are. Even in deep sleep you - as that Awareness - ARE - and that is clear in knowing "I was asleep, now I am awake". That Beingness, which some call Ordinary Awareness, is nonconceptual, indescribable, yet cannot be asserted OR denied! Know this as your real Self. Then look into the space which is always right here right now, clear and empty, and see if the notion that you are a "me" (whether you think of that "me" as a body, a thought, or any other passing fancy) and see what is seen. A subtle believed-in thought-sense or feeling-sense "I am me" is at the core. That is the root cause. See if you can find any actual entity! This "removes the cause" (so to speak). Though there never was an actual cause, it was only assumed!

See the nonexistence of the cause and the effects cannot remain. Simply seeing that "me" thought AS a thought - with no substance or existence apart from pure awareness, in your immediate and direct experience. See that this "I" or "me" thought or feeling is just a passing arising-presence, hanging out for a time, and then fading away. It's just moving energy - and NOT what you are.

You are that timelessness in which all of this temporal appearance appears – it arises, from nowhere, has an apparent temporary existence, and subsides back into the nowhere. Take that No Where No Thing to be what you are. Because, it IS! You are not what you think, feel, perceive, or believe yourself to be! Nothing temporary is real! Your True Nature is behind and beyond and within and all around all appearances, thoughts, movements, feelings etc. - and even behind consciousness of being, and THAT True You is not a thing at all. In short, YOU are No Thing No Where. Unborn and ever free.

Q: This means that it's not getting what the thoughts running through it say it wants. If I'm just subjectivity then these thoughts are arising and arrange themselves in such a way that suffering happens. Are these statements accurate or am I (this body) misunderstanding what these folks are pointing to?

C: You are just thinking up more concepts here. But NO concept is accurate or true! Even to claim your nature as pure subjectivity is going back into concepts and ignoring the fresh and obvious presence of being - the Is-Ness before the words or sensations appear. Before the next thought or feeling happens YOU ARE. Staying put there is effortless.

All the effort and struggle to attain what you already always are is doomed to failure so why not just stop here and now and be the space, be the nonconceptual ... why go back into words? Just see that you are and that is beyond doubt, and notice what you NAME or LABEL yourself as is only a bunch of concepts based on the erroneous concept of a separate "me".

Recognizing that there is no person in the space cuts through all the endless spiritual concepts and beliefs by rooting out the appearing yet false "cause" of all suffering – the belief in a "me". Do some looking into these pointers, looking – NOT thinking about or reading about it. You are giving all those thoughts of an endlessly analytic mind way too much credibility here! It's all nonsense in the end game.

You are, and that is already direct, immediate and known. You are That. That is really about all there is to this stuff!

Q: You wrote I think, you were saying to see if the notion that you are a "me" is true.

C: That's right. It was a slip of the editor ('me') :-)

Here is the update: Then look into the space which is always right here right now, clear and empty, and see if the notion that you are a "me" (whether you think of that "me" as a body, a thought, or any other passing fancy) and see what is seen. See if that notion is true. I love that you caught that! Clearly you are looking and investigating with earnestness and sincerity. Good on ya.

Q: There is a sense that I'm looking for this entity. Then when I look for a looker there isn't a looker to be found.

C: Right. Then isn't it clear that there is nothing to be found and no-one to find nothing?

Q: And it ain't the body looking for this. It didn't look under the mattress or in drawers or anything. So it's the mind looking but that's not true either. What I call mind (what calls mind "mind"?) is just a stream of thoughts. There isn't a mind at all. Yet the thought I'm looking is persistent even if it's not clear what is looking and how can looking happen without a looker.

C: Drop that story and keep looking to see if you really are separate. The story of "me" is an addiction you must break. Without the core belief in "me" all thoughts and analysis are absolutely meaningless. It takes the core assumption "I am me" to make all that mental noise mean something; and it always seems to mean something about that "me", doesn't it?

Q: This is a horrible mind bleep.

C: If you say so! Why do you keep repeating a lie?

Q: So I believe I am me but how can there be belief without a believer.

C: There cannot. See this: That "me" IS "the believer"! Beliefs and believer arise together as what you can call the fixated self-centered ego identity. So this proves that the core believer – the me – is still not being directly challenged! Now look: if there is no believed-to-be-real "me-believer" to be found in the space that you are, then what does that say about all beliefs? And questions? And doubts? And all the poor me stories? Story and storyteller arise together. Doubts and doubter arise together. Me and mine. I and other. All language – and you ignore the space that You ARE - and then even worse you eat these mental noises, these thought-words - which makes you sick. You eat a cardboard picture cutout of the meal and wonder why your hunger is not satisfied. This is absolute IGNORANCE. The cure for ignorance is staring you right in the face. It's your own True Self, empty, clear and utterly obvious. But you stubbornly insist on maintaining your sense of self as a separate suffering clod of grievances complaining that the world will not devote itself to making you happy. I got news: The world doesn't care. Almost everyone is in the same boat - always focusing "what about me"? "When will I be free?"

Q: How can there be suffering without somebody suffering yet it is believed and seems to be happening?

C: There can be NO suffering without the BELIEF that you are a person who suffers, a "me" that is whining and griping about "poor me"! This is the end game, and the only player is you – the I AM of your own consciousness of being itself, PRIOR to this conceptual entity ('I'm ME') which you still defiantly assume is what you are.

This notion remains as your fixation only due to lack of firm and committed investigation. This is where the pointing stops and it becomes YOUR job to challenge that core assumption. All the while, YOU ARE.

You deny with words that wordless presence that is inescapable. The only issue is that you continue - despite all the warnings the Universe sends you - to take yourself to be your thoughts and feelings and to ignore the presence, the consciousness, the Awareness which IS the Reality. You are that reality and you deny it at your own peril!

Cut the story, cut the whining, cut the bullshit and REALLY LOOK into this. You never were this "defective person" you ASSUME you are.

Know the truth that sets you free: YOU ARE and YOU KNOW YOU ARE. ALL else is bullshit! That is really all we point out here.

Follow-up (After a phone consultation)

Q: I'm looking at this notion that I am this body to see if it's true. Where this notion totally breaks down is that I am aware of the sensations and images that make up this "body". This "body" is totally made up of images and sensation and thoughts like "these thoughts are inside this body" or "this body is or I am suffering." I am aware of all these things or thoughts so how could I be one of them? That's where the belief in "I am this body" breaks down. So it's a start.

Thank you for the help. I'll keep in touch.

C: Okay!

I Exist - Is That TRUE?

This is another one that bears repeatinng... Q: Sometimes I realize I exist (not the conceptual I) and in those moments things are sweet and nice and what is is! It's like waking up to a beautiful dawn (of course there is no one to wake up). However, suddenly there is suffering and I am back to the little I being ME. I am back to seeking, etc.

C: But where IS this I"? In deep sleep "you" are not there, yet the life of that organism lives without your being there at all. The exact same is happening in the waking and dreaming states, with the trivial exception of a thought coming and going, which out of insecurity or fear we attach to and identify with. That "I" thought DOES represent something. What does that "I" point to? Undeniably, YOU ARE and prior to any thought, that existingness IS. It's the most obvious clarity. Overlooking that in favor of a thought story of an I is the cause of all suffering.

Q: I have been baffled as to how you do self inquiry. I know you can ask, 'who am I' but I still am unsure if it's an intellectual question or if it's something to drop into presence during still moments. After reading the chapter on, "how do I do self inquiry" in your book "Paradise Found", I asked myself, "who's asking", and then tried going deeper but I come down to being just IT or the BRAIN. This is where I get stuck. There is the sense that I am the brain and operating consciously from that and observing its thinking. Any ideas?

C: Read your own message again. Watch your own mind go I-I-I-I-I-I! Listen to your "little self-identity" and look right now: Is it real? Or is it a THOUGHT? Can a thought do anything? That "I" cannot really do self inquiry! How could a thought find it is not real? It's tail chasing. Where is an "it" or a "brain" without words, concepts? All of which just come and go in Infinite Awareness, which you cannot "know" because you ARE That...

Settle in with the pointers rather than try to "do" your way out. There is ultimately NO way out for a "you" that is unreal to start with! That said, if some inquiry or whatever comes up by itself, fine. This is not about rejecting practice, nor about the "I" understanding its true nature. The "I" doesn't HAVE a "true nature"!

Again WHERE is this separate entity with the label "I" that "gets stuck"?

There is no one in there so who would "do" some "practice"? Look at this: When you assume that what you are is a limited finite person, that you represent in language as "I", "me", you reinforce that assumed identity by taking up this or that practice to perfect this finite persona. But if that practice assumes you are a separate identity how could that practice allow you to transcend that false persona? That is like turning the dirty cop in the precinct out to catch the dirty cop in the precinct. And yet it appears to happen. That's the paradox of this, which the mind cannot ever grasp because the "mind" is only a thought! Can a thought grasp thought?

Q: Also, I have been thinking of meeting you. I know you live far away (I am in MD) and was wondering if it is possible to meet you in person some day?

C: You are welcome to come any time. However there may be no particular advantage in a face to face ... I found on meeting John Wheeler that his writings were actually more potent in a way owing to the absence of perceptive distractions! But I am still always happy to hang out with John; he is a great guy.

Shall we keep this real simple? You say "I exist" but in actual FACT, can you find, in REAL and actual nonconceptual experience, any such existing entity? This is a deeper look into this. Where is any I that exists - ACTUALLY? In simply terms, "you" do NOT exist. Yet existence appears as all of this - space and apparent content of space - in the timeless Dream Of Oneness.

The final question sometimes appears as "who is asking 'who am I'?" But that question has NO answer. That blankness you describe IS the actuality of infinite being, infinite space, infinite love.

Who or what is claiming a flip flop, me-and-BE? These are but energy arising as thoughts in Silence and these are never apart from The Silence, are they? This Silence is the Heart, the Substrate, of Consciousness, arising as that life force that makes the body live. Your problem is that you persist in identifying Consciousness as that body-brain-mind machine with it's, thoughts, feelings, experiences, senses, and perceptions. Of course again we come to a paradox: You don't do that! If you were doing it you would assuredly STOP doing it as it brings suffering!

So WHO or WHAT IS doing all this? That is the unanswerable question. Ask YOUR SELF, "What is That which I don't know that I don't know"?

Ponder this from Sri Nisargadatta Maharaj: "What makes you consider yourself a person [with its flip flops etc.]? Your identification with the body. Will this individual personality last? It will remain only so long as long as the identification with the body remains. But once there is a firm conviction that you are not the body, then that individuality is lost. It is the simplest thing, as soon as you have this conviction that you are not the body, then automatically, instantaneously, you become the manifest totality."

That manifest totality IS your Original nature, already complete and Presencing as the space-like Awareness IN which all that is manifest appears. The point being that Space and Its Content are of Single Essence - Aliveness arising from Nowhere and translated by language as I am, I exist.

Ponder this: You do not exist, and yet, YOU ARE. Nothing/Everything, Wisdom/Love.

And your Original Nature is that which is Prior to language. The closest language can come to That is, Being - What I don't know that I don't know.

Shock And Awe

Q: Hi Charlie, There was a recent shock in this mind-body organism as it was discovered that there is not the unborn and the born as two things.

C: Shocking indeed! But, to whom?

Q: Is it true that the unborn is also consciousness at play?

C: Conceptually, sure. Consciousness at rest, Consciousness in motion, are NOT TWO. Consciousness or Beingness IS all there is. But the concept ain't the reality of This Nondual Isness. Now: What is That which asks and what is That which answers? BOTH are only appearances in what is Real -- YOU are That in which question and questioner appears. So in this, there is no "truth" ... and all there IS is "truth". Not Two.

Q: It has been a pointer to see that there is an infinite context and then there is whatever is being experienced as the finite.

C. Finite and infinite are both this -- and neither is this. So – that is still linguistically just conceptual dualism. AKA bullshit, not to put too fine a point on it! You see, "Context" and "Content" are NOT Two. And in any case BOTH are merely concepts! This that is pointed to is that Understanding beyond concepts and THAT is the not-conceptual-natural-understanding that belongs to No One.

Q: What got knocked out was the perception that the unborn is emoting a play of form and function. This statement now seems separate. The unborn and the dream are "not-two."

C: So that IS cool! And, Not-Two, of course! But caution that the concept is NOT the actuality! So that is all okay so far as "language" goes, but THIS is prior to language -- it's sensed "here" that this is seen "there" by no-one, yes? But all this is just bubbles of Being - an appearance in (or as) what you are -- This Empty Presence. Yes? In any event it does sound like there was/is a sense of this timelessness – I describe this as a "dying before you die" to paraphrase the sage Bankei. Yes? But again for whom? :-)

Q: It was in the context of reading some Ramesh [the late Ramesh Balsekar]. There was also something said by him that spoke to that -- there is only pure functioning.

C: Yes. This is (as a pointer) the "functioning of Totality" but the concept is NOT what is pointed to by Ramesh, or this appearance, or any so called "other" in the guise of "teacher". Or "friend". By the way, utterly irrelevantly, "I" do adore the appearance called "Ramesh"!

Q: If this shift is one of truth then what else can be said about this?

C: Absolutely nothing. There is NO "truth" in THIS. Because "truth" is concept and THIS so-called "shift", which happens outside of time and to no-one, is Beyond Concept. That said, well -- welcome to the Home you never left!

Mind you, this can be a very common "experience" and the warning here is do not take ANY "experience" to be the Reality of what is pointed to. This is beyond concept and beyond experience. What does that leave? Nothing. Just That. That, No Thing, yet appearing as Every apparent Thing. THAT Thou Art!

Where is the doer in this appearance? There is NO shift, NO awakening, NO realization., NO "truth". All there is is ... all there is. That. Only That.

Communicating This Is Impossible, But...

When a self-centered "person" who is clinging and needy, wanting something from another -- whether that "other" is a "spiritual teacher or guide", or "revered guru type", or a "friend", or a "partner" -- then that selfish desire to "get something from you for me" creates a palpable toxicity that oozes through the communication like a noxious gas.

Most have experienced this through a clinging friend or lover who just would not leave you alone, who pestered and whined and was always wanting something from you. Sound familiar?

That is a result of a clinging to a false identity as an incomplete "me" always desiring more and more, the false person - that inauthentic phantom entity who wants something or needs help or affection or respect from others to feel whole out of the essential insecurity of being a flaming fake.

That fake will always seek to get something it believes it needs, from another taken to be most definitely "not me", who has what "me" wants and is withholding it, thereby making "me" unhappy. Then blaming starts!

And often a pitiful begging for some attention. But those appearances who want and need attention, or what they believe is love, from another, are doomed to much suffering - simply because you will never get enough to fill the ego's emptiness. It's a bottomless bucket you are trying to fill.

Who cannot see the futility in these clinging needs of a phantom?

All the lovers, gurus, teachers, friends or whatever in the world can no more put you right and whole than all the king's men could fix Humpty.

Why?

Because:

YOU (as a separate 'thing') simply DO NOT EXIST.

Yet, YOU ARE. Being. No Thing.

That is the paradox the mind can never resolve. Sit with that. When the paradox is held not as truth but as a pointer, the paradox dissolves (as does the mind). And the search ends in this dissolution. Right Now.

As Seng T'san put it in The Hsin Hsin Ming: "The wise man [or woman] strives to no goals but the foolish man [or woman] fetters himself. There is one Dharma, not many. Distinctions [and all desires] arise from the clinging needs of the ignorant."

The authentic expression of this true "Self-Knowledge" will often seem cruel and heartless to such "persons" who maintain that they are individuals and are convinced that the ones who share this directly - Heart To Heart, not "person to another person" - are sometimes just plain mean and have no empathy.

But that is the false persona-brain mentality interpreting what is and sticking whatever arises into it's maw of self-centered selfishness.

Seeking ANYTHING from a so-called "other" - whether that be solace, love, compassion, "spiritual help or coaching", peace, happiness, or attention and lovey-dovey words or hugs is a trap that may seem to provide a moment's peace but this peace is relative and very fleeting, as those who are barking up that wrong tree must finally discover.

The whole thing is a house of mirrors: there just are no "others". Sure, it does seem there are but looking deeper within yourself, finding there actually is no person with any actual substance or separate reality from Being Itself in "myself", is the final proof of this.

A reminder from a guy named Herbert Spencer fits here: "There is a principle which is a bar against all information, which is proof against all arguments and which cannot fail to keep a man [or woman] in everlasting ignorance--that principle is contempt prior to investigation". Don't overlook the potency in that one!

This proof consists in the dissolution of the utterly false belief in a person apart from others. It's that simple. You already ARE That in which all stories, doubts, questions and assumed persons appear. That is beyond language, indescribable, absolute, the One Subject or Source. All else is pretense and has no substance apart from Source.

This is ALL of One Taste, One Essence. Oneness, just That.

You are THAT in which it all appears. That is The Hard Truth & Ruthless Love That Sets You FREE.

Ask the mind: Who Am I that takes on board the odious idea of a me that is flawed and incomplete?

Who Am I? That thought reveals NO answer; it unconceals the Space, the Awareness, that You ARE.

Stay with THAT and let THAT show you the depths of Its emptiness and the richness of Its fullness.

All Appears IN and AS Aware Being-Aliveness

Q: I'm in and out of the story, sometimes; simultaneously in and out, usually more in than out, but I pride myself at how good I can be at nonconceptual awareness.

C: Wow. Pride! Which definitely 'goeth before' a FALL! And exactly who is going to EVER "be good at conceptual awareness"? You must see the infinite arrogance of that belief!

Q: Re: this "stay with the sense I am" [as pointed to by Sri Nisargadatta Maharaj] in the interest of hastening my death. If I think "nonconceptual awareness" or "bare-naked awareness" I can instantly do that and it feels detached and sometimes blissful, but if I think, "stay with I am" I feel like I'm stuck in the ego or that it's a thought loop that's getting in the way of non-conceptual awareness.

C: Whose death? What is that which was "born"? Only A thought! "I". And can a thought actually get in the way of Awareness? NO. Thoughts APPEAR IN Awareness. Like a cloud cannot affect the empty space of sky, a thought cannot actually touch or obscure Awareness. Now look: WHO "feels" or "thinks" these stories of a "me stuck"? You complain of ego. Show that ego to me! Look for an "ego". What is found?

C: Does this "self center" or "discrete point of view" actually exist? What is the so-called self center or point of view made of? And who views what from such a point of view? Where is this viewing point located - exactly? Does it have any actual substance apart from a sometimes thought or sensation or perception? Is there seeing there right now? What sees? What hears? What is the space IN which all that story of a "poor me" who is seeking some resolution to a problem that does not even exist apart from imagination appears? What ARE "you"? Are you a thing apart from this Seamless Timeless Whole? If so what is it made up of? Who says and thinks "I am separated and want to become whole"? The "assumed person ' you'" - are a fictional character pretending mightily against all evidence that you are real and apart and this is pure imagination. You take a thought of

I or ME on board and ASSUME you are that separate entity and that you have some power apart from the Universal Isness that is the Causeless Source of all that is and so "you" suffer. But it's all imagination; you are dreaming.

Ponder these words of Sri Nisargadatta's: "Watch yourself closely and you will see that whatever be the content of consciousness, the witnessing of it does not depend on the content. Awareness is itself and does not change with the event. The event may be pleasant or unpleasant, minor or important, awareness is the same. Take note of the peculiar nature of pure awareness, its natural self-identity, without the least trace of self-consciousness, and go to the root of it and you will soon realize that awareness is your true nature, and nothing you may be aware of, you can call your own.

"When the content is viewed without likes and dislikes, the consciousness of it is awareness. But still there is a difference between awareness as reflected in consciousness and pure awareness beyond consciousness. Reflected awareness, the sense "I am aware" is the witness, while pure awareness is the essence of reality. Reflection of the sun in a drop of water is a reflection of the sun, no doubt, but not the sun itself. Between awareness reflected in consciousness as the witness and pure awareness there is a gap, which the mind cannot cross".

Q: Also, you had a John Wheeler, so why can't I have a John Wheeler?

C: First off WHO is that "I" that wants ANYTHING other than what is right here right now? Investigate! Secondly: Look, if you want to have a John Wheeler point out what is real and what is not, why not write to John Wheeler and not Charlie Hayes? Go see him. Set up a consultation call with him!

Q: Will you be my John Wheeler?

C: NO. But I am happy to point out what is real and what is not. Which is precisely what John Wheeler will more than likely do if you meet or speak with him! In his own unique fashion. LOOK: Find the expression that resonates vibrantly for that "entity you assume is you" and stick with his or her pointers until there is no false assumed personal entity believed in any more, never, ever, and the search is done once and forever.

Q: I know that in non-conceptual awareness I'm already awake to some degree, but I'm definitely not dead, even though I could honestly say, "well, I'm not a seeker. I get it".

C: What is the nature of that "I" that claims "I'm already awake to some degree"? Can't you see the bullshit in that "entity claiming some attainment" and declares it has happened "to me" and "to some extent" all of which reinforces the belief in a me and time? Moreover, the assumption "I get it" very simply proves that you do NOT "get it". THERE IS NOTHING TO GET AND NO ONE TO GET NOTHING.

Q: This is all there is the one life happening only now, both dream and reality, the dream known, the reality unknown except that I am that reality and I allow that reality to run my life, beingness makes all my decisions, pretty much. Still, I'm definitely not dead. Thank you for You Tube and your videos.

C: Those "enlightened concepts we believe, and actually Being This, are night and day different. KEEP GOING. In Sri Nisargadatta's words, "The real exists and is of the nature of witness-consciousness. Of course it is beyond the witness, but to enter it one must first realize the state of pure witnessing.

"The awareness of conditions brings one to the unconditioned. We can talk only of the unreal, the illusory, the transient, the conditioned. To go beyond, we must pass through total negation of everything as having independent existence. All things depend on consciousness. And consciousness depends on the witness".

Awareness of Being is Timeless Bliss, Perfect Peace... now looking within your own Consciousness, ask YOU - WHO is aware of Being?

And WHO or WHAT is this "I" you claim to be yourself that "assumes" this or that? You see, that I ITSELF is a mere assumption made in ignorance; that "I" thought has no actual substance, and zero independent power, and in Truth that "seperate I" does NOT exist. Yet EXISTENCE IS. The conceptual "I" POINTS to Timeless Being and when that concept is taken to be me there is much suffering. The cure is to see that phantom "I" *as* a phantom!

YOU as what you "know yourself as" are a nonexistent phantom, a ghost of wispy thought with no capacity to do or not do, to be or not be, a damn thing.

Q: So I practice "Who am I?" And keep thinking "maybe the next video or rewatching the last one will tell me more about how to ask this question". I know I'm everything and nothing and not a person, yet I'm completely ignorant as to the experience. Who am I? I assume if I ask this question in silence something is going to pop up some day and that will be that.

C: This is NOT an "experience"! Awareness is NOT a thought or a feeling, not a perception or a sensation! As to "your doing", you will do the next thing. The immeasurable forces that comprise Being, Consciousness, Aliveness – Life Itself, Totality, will push that organism and the assumed entity to the next thing with no struggle or effort. If the assumption remains operational under the covers, like DOS code under the Windows graphical appearance, that "you" must "figure this out" and "get some attainment someday" then ask WHO believes this? WHO AM I?

The question "who am I" is NOT asked to get any answer or any attainment. To paraphrase Sri Ramana Maharshi´s words: The thought, the unaswerable question, "who am I"?, will destroy all other thoughts, and in the end, that thought itself will also be destroyed, like a stick used to stir a fire is also burnt up in the end. To dissolve the false belief in being a separate entity that must manage and create and exert some will or intention and try (and ALWAYS fail) to make it's life work – and the fact is that belief in being a "me" IS the root cause of all suffering. Remove the cause (that false belief in a seperated "me") and can the effects remain? No. that final question asked relentlessly is a simple means that many have found just flat works.

If that doesn't work keep looking. This pathless path is made in the walking which NO ONE does. Everything is One Essence appearing as nothing and everything and the whole show between.

Stay simple and be in touch is spirit so moves that happening in This Awareness that is Real. Good luck and much love!

WHO Claims "I Am Afraid?

Q: I have a ton of fear at the moment (actually have had it my whole life, developing into "anxiety disorder" about 11 yrs ago) and its getting worse.

C: Let me say right away, Nonduality is NOT a substitute for any body or mind-brain disorders. The proper place to deal with that issue is with a qualified medical professional. If you are not currently getting that kind of assistance, please do so as soon as you can.

Q: I watch the silliness of the mind and I view the whole thing as "allowing a thorn to remove a thorn" or "the mind destroying itself". Are these descriptions apt?

C: All descriptions are just that – descriptions of some happening or some concept. What we point out here is that NO description is "apt" OR "not apt".

Q: In addition, you talk about "breathing into the fear" and "letting it come", and you also elude to your battles with intense fear before your "awakening" in other audio/videos - could you elaborate on these 2 things more for me please.

C: Prior to my meeting John Wheeler I was sometimes afraid of a future that never came and I realized finally that all "my fears" were only and always about a "me" that was believed to be real and solid, as an entity, and the basic lament of that egoic entity is "what will happen to 'me' if this or that terrible future happens?" When this "me" sense was investigated it was found to be substantially nonexistent, merely a chimera or appearance of thought energy taken to be solid and seperate in ignorance. That points to the clear seeing that in fact "the me" does not exist. and yet, I AM – whole, complete, and existing here and now as Being, Consciousness, Aliveness Itself.

Prior to meeting John Wheeler, I took a course developed by an Indian sage, one Sri Sri Ravi Shankar (no relation to the famous Sitar player), called The Art Of Living. In this course I learned a series of physical yogic practices, manly centered on the breath, that made a difference in the body-mind apparatus with the name

Charlie. Some habitual fears seemed to be "imbedded" in the brain and body cells from race car crashes and a few other "near death" happenings (one of which was nearly drowning in a wild ocean surf and getting a breath at the very last instant when the breath could be held no longer.)

Given the experience this organism had I recommend that course without reservation, particularly for those with chronic anxiety or fear, but ONLY with the concurrence of your health professional. Check it out at www.artofliving.org and then check with your doctor about whether it may be of benefit for you.

Q: Thank you! To be honest, I don't know how much more fear and silliness this mind can put up with before it explodes or something. Your help is much appreciated.

C: No worries. Just follow the pointers as best you can and do make sure you are getting good support from appropriate sources, and please ponder the pointers that follow below, to nail down the FACTS (NOT Assumptions!) of what you are and what you are not. You may also find asking yourself, who Am I? Who is claiming "I" am afraid or anxious? As Sri Ramana Maharshi put this, "The thought 'who am I' will destroy all other thoughts and in the end that thought will itself be destroyed, like a stick used to stir a burning fire is itself destroyed in the end ..."

If there is a sense of longing for love, happiness or peace, a feeling of needing to locate a truth, a sense of something still missing or something wrong:

You must resolve the core issue of your REAL "self-identity" right from the start. Knowing what you are - and also knowing what you are not - is essential to realizing the natural state of your true Being. One pointer is to challenge all you "know" and see directly you are NOT what you know you are, NOT anything you can name or see or realize. Knowing what you are not - not that thought, not this feeling, not that perception, not this knower, not that "mind", not that seer, not that hearer, not ANY thing; not that body not any words not any such this or that – is certainly one approach - but this way of looking alone will not necessarily give the final push into the already realized Eternal State.

One can spend a whole lifetime on self-inquiry, yoga, study of scriptures, meditation, worship, breathing practices, or any other path of "becoming" – which depends in itself on a falsely assumed "time" or "someday" - and end up with nothing more than extreme frustration, unless the core issue of authentic identity is resolved out of the gate.

Do you know what you really are?

Get THAT handled first. What are you? Undeniable and Undefined, Unborn, Being.

YOU ARE. Any doubt about that? Awareness IS. IN that Awareness there IS Consciousness, direct incontrovertible KNOWING, translated by language ("mind") as I AM.

Any question that Awareness IS and there IS Consciousness arising here and now?

You – the Authentic You – Are that Awareness and nothing else. Everything that appears, appears IN (or ON) this empty screen of Pure Awareness. You are That. Get that beyond doubt. Even doubts arise in or on that Awareness. Understand – You Are That. Nothing but That. Full stop.

Pause thought in this instant and here you are, not as a thought, just ordinary wakefulness which is in fact no thing – you are no thing and yet, YOU ARE. Existing as Consciousness, and prior to Consciousness abiding eternally as Being-Aware-Of-Itself and THAT is peace, the Bliss of Simply Being. This is the Bliss That Is – and yet belongs to no-one.

Tat Tvam Asi. THAT, Thou Art. Sat-Chit-Ananda. Awareness-Awakeness-Lovingness.

Stormy Weather? In this Awareness-Consciousness there appears moving Energy-Aliveness, appearing as all manner of experiencing, all of which is like stormy or calm weather, windy or calm, rainy or sunny, weather appears in the empty sky yet the sky itself remains empty, free, untouchable and invincible. Like that YOU as Being-Awareness are that empty sky of apparent Consciousness, silently observing and also permeating the objective appearance, the storms and calms of anxiety, fear, joy, happiness, love, hate, and all the mental movements out of a silence so vast no sound can ever obliterate it.

There Is No Other Than That.

The So Called "Flip-Flop"

Q: It seems that the seeing is clear, especially when talking to another person about this kind of thing. The ego sense seems to come back at times and is felt as a very tight contraction, with a lot of "thoughts about me." It seems as though there is no problem, until I come in and try to run the show, or try to figure things out. Sometimes there is a sense of desperation to end the seeking, which can turn into self-seeking or self gratifying behaviors.

C: Ramesh Balsekar calls this appearance the "flip-flop" – a useful metaphor, as it seems (but ONLY seems) that some "entity-called-me" asserts itself as language, words, thoughts of a separate person with some ownership of the appearance (this is MY life, MY words MY etc etc.).

Q: Is it simply a matter of letting the seeking fizzle out?

C: The pointer is to keep looking for the "I" that would "let" ANYTHING happen. That "I" is merely a conceptual and utterly fictional storyteller telling the story of an I. Have a look and see what is "writing" and what is "playing out" the story of I or me? In a separate "world out there"? Where is the "author"? You are dreaming and in the dream you are dreaming that there is a way to wake yourself up from the dream. (To mix a few metaphors).

Q: Trying to end the search seems futile, as well as trying to just be a "regular person" and ignore the revealings or insights that have come. It seems like there is something that has to happen, some final seeing of the false.

C: This expectation of some "final event" is one of the many myths that seem to say there IS a person and there IS a "special state" that this fictional person can attain in an imaginary something called "a future". But this set of suppositions is all imagination, assumptions, and ignores the timeless Being that is the Reality PRIOR to language. "You" as a person apart simply do not exist. YOU as What You ACTUALLY Are is That Being which NEVER changes. To ignore this Beingness and consider your self to be a thing in time is the one and only mistake that gets corrected in clear seeing from and into Naked Awareness.

Q: Different teachers all have different messages and trying to decipher them with concepts is pointless.

C: Then what makes you keep doing that? Look into that. What Power makes you YOU and makes that you seek to end seeking? Where is the source of seeking, what is that which gives the organism life? What is the SOURCE of your very ALIVENESS?

Q: The actual seeing seems to be the only real thing, the fundamental awareness. Does the looking require some sort of maintenance, like a daily regime?

C: That makes Awareness into an object! This Awareness is the unchanging background to all appearance and needs no "maintaining" – look, where does awareness begin? Where is awareness located? What is looking and thinking and judging? That which is apparently "doing" all that is NOT awareness, it's a witnessing judging false entity that appears and disappears IN awareness.

Q: In the absence of conscious looking it seems as though the ego sense goes unnoticed until the suffering becomes too severe, at which point the looking seems to happen more intensely.

C: That is a story the false author tells to survive and that is just plain bullshit.

Q: Is there any choice in this?

YES. NO. Both answers are stories and FALSE. LOOK for yourself, see if "you" HAVE any choice in Reality. WHO claims to choose or claims to have no choice? You have got to do the work, not just get "an answer" from some imaginary author teacher guru etc!

Q: Being in bondage to this seems unbearable, just wanted to hear your thoughts. Thank you very much, there is something undeniably real here, if only I could just die already.

C: What was born that now wants to die? Find that one to be a chimera, a cloud-like non-entity, and the search ends. Are you looking or merely playing the concept game? Staying in concepts and trying to figure this out will leave you utterly frustrated. Come back to that which is certain and real, Being Itself. That Being is No thing. It appears as things but these things are not actually solid and real as physics has now shown. You are NO thing.

Ponder this from John Wheeler:

Awareness is self-evident and easily known, even now. Not by a "someone". The someone idea is a concept. What you are is prior to concepts. The person comes afterwards as an appearance in awareness. Awareness is prior to the notion of the "I". Hearing is happening; no one is hearing; later we say "I" hear, but that "I" thought is not present in the hearing, only in the subsequent labeling. All experience is "I"-less, or impersonal. What you are cannot be seen as a "thing apart" because you cannot become an object to yourself. All the problems come from trying to conceive of your being as something objective, which it is not. You are, no doubt. But being is not a thing, which is why we overlook it and identify with an object. Settle in with the awareness-presence, and whatever its characteristics are, naturally become evident. That is already present, but overlooked. Just as being and awareness are ever-present but often not recognized, so is the non-suffering and unchanging freedom of your ever-present true self. I can only point; it is up to you to see it for yourself.

Follow-up:

Q: Thanks Charlie, this was quite helpful. I appreciate your on-point response, and continuous patience.

C: De nada :-).

What IS Fear?

Q: It has been a number of months since our last exchange, things have become clearer to me, I've been re-reading John Wheeler's pointers.....always very helpful. The reason why I am writing you again is that there is an apparent obstacle in the form of great, annihilating fear when I relax in the present and it's seems to become bigger the more relaxation happens. I let it happen and accept as best as I can but the fear persists and is coming back again and again for months now and has me stuck somehow with it. Of course it is not real - however it feels very real in these particular moments. Do you have any "hands-on" advice or comment about this "obstacle". As always your efforts on line with all of your pointers are very much appreciated!

C: Thanks. Now: You say "I" let it happen, and "I" accept as best "I" can but what exactly IS this "I"? Moreover what is this that you call fear? What are these things called "I" and "fear" MADE of? What is their substance? Are these things at all?

What Is A "Me"?

We say this is me, you know me or you don't know me, we say this is mine and that is not mine – all as though this me or I that claims to be "myself" is a THING.

Okay, fair enough. But what IS the "thing" you and I call "me"?

If "me" is a thing, what is that thing made of?

Things have properties and are made of some essential thing; like snow is made of water, like wind is made of air, like the appearing text, images and white space on your computer screen is made of ones and zeros, like the images on the page are made of ink, like the rug is made of wool. So what exactly is "me" made of? What is the essence, the fundamental or "elemental" nature if you like, of a "me"?

Do you know that in actual fact, you do not know? Is it clear that while we say me and mine, as though we are a thing that owns other things, that we do not know what that me-thing really is?

194

And if we don't know what it is how do we know there really IS a "thing called me"?

Again I ask us, what is this me made of? Can we describe this me as we might describe a cloud (well, it's puffy, white and gray, sort of semi-transparent, and it's changing shape slightly as I look at it)?

Describe your "me" right now. How is it described? Who is that doing the describing? Isn't that "me" describing "me"? Isn't "me" going around in circles – me describes me – and what is the describer? The knower of this me describing me? What proves the existence of this me? Isn't it all a self-reference, energetically and convincingly proving it is real by referring to itself as a thing apart from all other things, over and over? Some call that a vicious circle of conceptual thought referring to a self-avowed existence filled with an energy of emotions, feelings, and desires (always desiring what is NOT present already, present here and now, wanting or fearing a "future" and damning or desiring a "past"). Isn't that just another description? What is that description made of?

Look into your own sense of being a me. Look directly without attempting to alter that me, or change it in any way. Does that bring up some "fear"? What is that which is afraid? What IS "fear"? Other than energy with a concept labeling it? Whose "energy" is that? Now see if this me is an "it" at all. Is your sense of me an object with properties? Is that me really an object and does it call itself the subject? Isn't that idea of a subject observer of other objects or even other subjects actually substantial? If you say it is then tell me what it is made of, what IS its substance? Be precise.

Again what is that seeming "subject-me" made up OF? What is its essence? Be precise in describing the essence of this me. For example: "This ME -- it is a bubble of energy, it is a membrane of sorts, a veil, between nothing and the world, it's a sensation, a vibration -- it's a – ummm – I cant really nail down its properties, but I know it is and it's me – what is it made of? I guess I have to admit I don't really know what me is made of –

oh but wait, me is this body, solid, real, apart from all the other bodes, all the other objects – what is the body made of? What is the essence of this body"?

Look into the body and see what it consists of. Water, air, earth (food), fire (heat), these are the essential properties or substance of the body, right? But what is all of THAT made of? Isn't it all energy imbued with a subtle intelligence that allows that energy to form a beating heart, a brain with the knowing of how to walk, how to speak? Now what is the substance of that which observes, describes, and defines itself as that body?

That is more difficult to nail down, isn't it?

Have a good look! What is ME made up of?

This body? Omigod -- body and all those descriptions of its essence ... just thoughts! Me? I'm just a thought! A thought! An idea of being. Is the idea of being really my being? If so then I am born and I die every few moments as I don't know I am me unless I happen to think about me! Am I a thought? What is a thought made of? Now we're back to the beginning of this ponderation! What is a me? A thought form, forming a self-image, a picture show with sounds and images. Self image! Image – is an image of a thing the actual thing? Is the movie on the screen made of real solid characters and buildings and cars and trees etc? What is the movie made of? What is the screen made of? What about the light that illuminates it all? What is that light made of?

What is a thought form made of other that light and shadow? What is LIGHT made of? What!?

WHO CARES?

What's for lunch?

Q: Thank you for your reminder, "I" took something for real which is not and, as anything unreal, the fear has passed and it can or will come back, but that's irrelevant - what is important is that what is real... Your collection of pointers snapped me right out of that dream - I needed that slap to "sober up" :-)

From John Wheeler's recent pointers:" The only issue is — do you know beyond any doubt whatsoever what you are? Also, is there any tendency to believe in yourself as a separate self apart from reality? If either of these points is not clear, the suffering and doubts will go on, no matter what else is understood and how clearly the pointers are expressed or understood at a verbal level." It's time to stop playing around and to know once and for all what I am! Hey, it's way too easy for my "sophisticated" mind - LOL. Let me steam with that.............. Thank you so much.

C: You are very welcome. Stay in touch, as Oneness moves that happening.

Watching The Magic Show Called 'Life'

Follow-up from J...

J: Everything is really evening out! I owe you the credit for the final push, although on a deeper level there is total understanding that "you" did not do anything and "I" had nothing to understand because neither one of us exists!! That does bring deep peace, who is there to feel guilty, judge people, hold grudges, worry about wrong decisions yada yada yada, when there are NO PEOPLE doing anything, no decisions have ever been made on any level and no mistakes, accidents, tragedies, etc, EVER because WHO WOULD THEY HAVE HAPPENED TO?

Everything is a divinely orchestrated masterpiece dancing to infinitely perfect intelligence, we (whatever that means) THE AUDIENCE OF NONE simply watch it all unfold NOW

MAGIC!!!!!!!

C: Thanks for this great good news!

As John Wheeler says, "Settle in with the awareness-presence, and whatever its characteristics are, naturally become evident. That is already present, but overlooked. Just as being and awareness are ever-present but often not recognized, so is the non-suffering and unchanging freedom of your ever-present true self. I can only point; it is up to you to see it for yourself".

All any "expression" of this can do is point. You did the looking and now the fruits are here. Congratulations! Love ya.

On The Path To Nowhere

Q: I just wanted to say that the newsletter totally rocks. It all makes perfect sense and fits in to where I am with no adjustment.

I am on the path of self discovery and your newsletter brings clarity to my experience. The conversation is amazing and resonates with all that I am. Thank you. Keep up all the great efforts to remind us humans that we are free and that there is no where to go, nothing to do. Love to you.

C: This is great to hear! Sounds like the pointers are settling in. Meanwhile, if doubts or questions arise, or if there is still an assumed belief that there is "a me on a path", look deeply into the space - where does this assumed "I" arise from? That Empty Naked Being is YOU; while the "I" is a thought and is not What You Are ... YOU are That Awareness prior to consciousness, which appears here and now as the sense of being "I am". Seeing this once and for good ends the notions of seeking, seeker, and any path. Then it is clear that all paths lead away from Paradise and the Home you never left is right here, right now.

Q: What you write is true and I'm grateful for your clarity. Paradise is right here but at the moment thoughts take my awareness out of the stillness. So my practice is to experience this peace on more of a constant basis as I know this is the only place that exist. Thanks for your correspondence. Love, P.

C: Awareness is NOT a belonging, NOT AN OBJECT! And "you" cannot EVER either attain OR escape this Awareness ... it is YOU ... this is simply the Eternal; Beingness that IS - this Spacelike Awareness belongs to NO one. In short, it ain't YOUR Awareness; it is just ... empty Ordinary Non-conceptual Presence-Awareness. You do not need to practice to BE. YOU ARE. THAT is the incontrovertible indestructible Eternal Awareness.

Don't confuse personal consciousness of "stuff" with Timeless BEING-Awareness!

C: thank you Charlie. I love your passion and focus

C: You are very welcome. Stay in touch, as Oneness moves you to do that. Meanwhile ponder: Where does this "sense of being a me, a personality" come from? See what is seen, and notice that all this that appears, appears in the Eternal Non-conceptual Impersonal Being-Awareness that you truly are.

That is the beginningless timeless ever-fresh true nature of this Isness - arising right here and right now, whatever "time" the clocks say it is and wherever "you" apparently are, as Living Aliveness Itself.

No Thing in Essence, Every Thing is Appearance. Ocean and Waves.

But:

Can something come from no thing?

WHAT did the mind say?

How could a thing come from no thing?

Everything is nothing.

Or, nothing is everything.

Neither statment is true. Nor are they false.

Reunion

What Is Reality?

Being-Knowing is all there is.

But "IS" requires "Is Not!"

What is it that is PRIOR to both Is and Is Not?

What is That Eternality which "allows" for BOTH the Is and Is Not?

What is Real? Permanent? Forever? (Forever is not a "really long '"time").

What IS Forever and NOT in or bound up with "time"? Space? Distance? What might THAT be?

What is forever is, Is-Not".

Reality Is Not and also IS?

"What is NOT, Is. What Is, is Not". ~ John Greven

You Cannot NOT BE

In all this 'time' have you EVER stopped BEING? Isn't being itself always here, always now? Don't overlook the profundity of that seeing, that obviousness! Being is EASY; it already IS.

Q: Easy? It's taking an awful long time (yes, I know, time doesn't exist) for me.

C: If you really know deep down that "time does not exist" then what is your problem with "taking a long time"? The mind tries to have its cake and eat it too. This is delusion, time is or is not! Can't have it both ways, my friend.

THIS that IS was never not obvious, only overlooked. There is NO ME, not anywhere anywhen. All there is is Being, the Seeing-Knowing prior to the mind-translation. Look for a "me" and you will never find one. Listen to the Podcasts on http://beingisknowing.blogspot.com and get under the minds false assertions before you make such sweeping claims about that which you cannot grasp

Q: Someone else said recently, to his questioner, "Work on noticing that space between your thoughts, be there with your awareness, a deep breath, and awe; in that space time stands still and the " I am" that you came into life with will smile at you! In that vast empty space, you will smile at the freedom and emptiness of it. The clouds of thought will disappear but still be there, but the space between them grows."

C: Okay, lovely. But lets take apart the last assumption in this ... the "doer" who now would "work on it".

WHO is gonna "work on noticing the space between thoughts etc"? That is yet another totally futile practice that just reinforces the UTTERLY FALSE idea of a seeker who needs to do something to BE what is already clearly present and obvious! Such teacher/teaching is a disservice. Being already IS and everything/everyone IS THAT. There is nothing to "attain", simply because there is no ACTUAL seeking-entity to be found on direct evidence. So all this noise seemingly keeps the false in place seemingly looking for that which already is.

Q: My only point being is that some people really struggle with the endless mind chatter! And a lot of people I've met have a very big struggle with the concept of the fact that there is no duality in non-duality, that Being is, always will be and that we cannot but be THAT. I was just throwing out a baby step. Full Stop! There is nothing to argue.

C: Okay. No worries. But these statements do contradict. What "people" "you" have met? What "you is that which makes claims of knowing then denies that very knowing in the next breath!?

I'm not having a go at anyone personally here; just pointing out how the mind will delude itself (and I am NOT saying you are deluded here ... it may well be that the search is done and your pointing is just out of love and compassion. That is all to the good as far as I am concerned!

And at the same (no) time, if there no duality in nonduality there is no "other person" and no "you" to "meet" such "others". Who gives "baby steps" to WHOM? This is the mind's delusion. You cannot have it both ways, The absolute is not sometimes people and sometimes not. There is no grey here. It is black and white, or "Black Letter Law". That Law is that Being IS. ONLY Being-Knowing IS. There are no "others". You parrot the words but your expression shows there is still a subtle believed-in "believer" that has not yet fully disappeared. Everyone is THAT full stop. Sure, out of a sense of "gratitude" expressions happen. But Oneness WILL pounce on a misleading point. No one does that. It simply HAPPENS. All good.

Thoughts appear and disappear. What YOU are is NOT a thought, yet thoughts appear. So what? To "try to notice" or "get a gap" is just bullshit so don't get wrapped up in yet another futile practice. YOU ARE. Being. Just THAT. Inescapable and undeniably HERE NOW. NO practice can "reveal" your True Nature. You ARE this Being-Presence. So drop all that and simply BE as you already are. Full Stop!

How Will I Know When I'm Done?

C: Simple answer: When there is no longer that question or its apparent questioner.

But wait ... Who wants to know? WHAT "I"? WHO wants to know "how long?" Who cares? Who asks that question? Take a good look! Where is the questioner, the thinker?

No one knows "I am done". It is obvious when the Understanding is coming from the FACT that there IS no "one" to either be done or not done! Another simple answer? When that question no longer has any reality. Or when the question no longer appears, to put it another way... just recognize right now that this question ... and the questioner ... appear together, as those mental brain-sounds, which are intrinsically meaningless. So in the Seeing, Being, the questions, doubts, and suffering simply are no more. They were never actually real and they are not real here and now.

Here and now YOU ARE ... being, just That and nothing else! There's no way can you deny THAT.

Let that sink in. When there is no such question taken seriously, then, even as NOW, Life is JUST HAPPENING. The "I" you still accept as you is a phantom, a fake, it's the emperor strutting in his imaginary finery onto the stage. But he's actually buck naked. You are that: Bare Naked Awareness-Presence. ALL those ideas that claim otherwise are nonsensical beliefs. Merely false assertions!

We have visited several times. Now all your questions have been answered over and over when we have talked; you have called several times and the pointers have been delivered. You have gotten the anti-virus injection.

But the mind's stubbornness (which is not unusual so don't get all down about it) is keeping the clear seeing at bay. You must get some willingness and earnestness together somehow to really get after this and end the bullshit once and for all. Defeat that stubborn hanging-on to concepts. NO concept is real. None!

Life is just happening ... to no one. You are Life Itself! Just do not give the mental lies any credence! And stop refusing to be what You are. That's it, my friend. Full Stop, as 'Sailor' Bob Adamson says.

Keep after this. Give it a good few hours a day! And stay in touch as the Spirit moves you to. I Love You.

Follow-up:

Q: I'll get real with this and listen to the audios today. Yes, you're right, all of my questions have been answered and any question coming up is a refusal to see what is. Love, Mr. x.

C: Bang ON. Love ya back.

Where is Time?

Q: For a long time, there was no longer any interest in the search [for 'enlightenment'] and there wasn't even much tendency to evaluate what that means.....

C: Where is any 'time' without thoughts? Time is a concept and NOT real. Only this Presence, this immediacy we call 'now', is actually REAL.

Q: There were odd related thoughts like, "so is this it? .....now what?....where is the bliss?"

C: Bliss is what You ARE. That is another name for What IS. Call it Love, Peace, Bliss, or Dogcrap! The label is NOT the REAL. There is no word for what you are. Period!

THAT ... your ACTUAL Being-Presence ... is always here, always now, and never NOT. We miss it by seeking some imaginary 'state' for the 'seeker" that "I hope I gain 'someday!'". What is not clear is the first pointer, to what is REAL ... the Fact Of your indisputable Being Itself. There is no time, doubt, suffering or any 'someday' in That. You are THAT.

Don't miss, or dismiss, the basic point of this, that as has been said in a trillion ways, you already are what you seek, and what misses that simple point? What are you looking for? What you are looking FROM. The only FACT is your actual timeless Being, and THAT is Love, Peace, whatever label. It is a warm open Presence that is right here along with all these thoughts, feelings, and notions of time and someday.

That Presence, that "bliss" or Endless beginningless Is-ness, is with you always, AS You.

Q: ...still these questions were seen to arise and fade and did not bring suffering....but today brought old familiar feelings of guilt mainly, from which D. has a long history....guilt about perceived laziness, non-doing, drinking too much....

I guess what I'm trying to say is that this recurrence of negativity surprised me and the things teachers say has become predictable and of little help....help which I thought was no longer needed anyway, but just today there is misery....

C: And yet that can never touch or effect that Timeless Absolute Presence, can it? See for yourself! That Presence is simply NEVER missing but overlooking that to focus on imagined "problems or issues" it gets ignored (and that's what is called self-ignorance). The Self already IS, and cannot be gained OR lost. It's YOU. The cure for self-ignorance is this Self-Knowledge. Don't skip over the profound possibility in that!

Q: Seeing who I'm not doesn't seem to make a difference on the quality of the story.....??

C: That is usually the case, that "seeing who I am not" doesn't quite hit home, because the issue of what you ARE has not been clarified.

Give the Podcasts on the blog a few good listens, especially 'Sailor' Bob's and John Wheeler's ones. Look at what is Present always, get to know That.

I Love You. Thanks for writing; stay in touch if you like.

Only Not-A-Thing Is Real

See if you can find anything that is NOT an object appearing to what You are. Even the assumed subject-I is simply another object appearing to what You are. What you are is not any object. You are That Eternal Being to which ALL objective appearance appears. What never comes and goes? YOU. From the start not a thing IS. And YOUbare that not-a-thing.

ONLY not-a-thing IS.... ! Forever.

Ever watch a great movie or TV show and get so immersed you totally forgot about yourself? Did that show seem like reality? They call some shows "realty TV". But what IS "reality? We get immersed in the movie and that seems to be reality. Then after the movie is finished, we get immersed (or re-immersed) in another movie called "life'. "My life, my world". But unlike the TV or film show we simply have forgotten that what we call "reality' is NOT REALLY REALITY.

Let's say our definition of Reality is That which NEVER changes. Doesn't the "movie of me and world" change constantly? The big mistake we make is to "lay up our treasure where moth and rust doth corrupt".

To take on the false idea of me and then assume that this "me concept" is what I am and this appearance of me/world is reality is, to put it rather bluntly, to have our head where it is dark and stinky. Who cannot see this?

Once the Reality dawns that there is no real time, real world, real me, real other, then the whole house of cards built up over the always changing foundation of a persona tumbles. The foundation is seen as a house made of words that never meant anything at all. And life lives itself in freedom and peace ... as it ever was, ever is, and ever shall appear to be!

So listen up. The Podcasts by 'Sailor' Bob, John Wheeler, and John Greven are the most potent I have ever heard for dismantling the house of cards and leaving you as simply naked Being, only That.... living in freedom as the natural, eternal isness.

Go for it, my friends. All you have to lose is a false "persona-you" that never gave you anything but endless suffering interspersed with momentary but temporary release when some goal was achieved. And no achievement ... no matter how "profound or special" ... has ever given you the peace and joy you have craved since forever, has it? Let's be honest with ourselves.

It seems earnestness is required. While there is no one to "be earnest" earnestness can definitely arise.

Let it be so. Let it be so NOW. For YOU.

I Love You.

Birth and Death Appear In Life Itself

Q: will you explain what happens when the body-life ends?

C: Who asks this question?

What is that "I" that wants an answer to an unanswerable question? Who has been to that "undiscovered country from whose bourn no traveler returns"?

Look down below the question to locate the birthless deathless Source, the Eternal Is-Being that NEVER changes. It is THAT in which consciousness (birth) and no-consciousness (death) APPEARS. Bodies come and go. The subject/object assumption appears in That. That ...YOU as-You-are ... remains always, shining in luminous non-conceptual Isness. That Eternal Reality is YOU: Reality beyond birth and death.

Consciousness of being is what is called birth. Reality of Being before consciousness is Life Itself. YOU are Life Itself. There is NO such thing as death! LIFE is beginningless, endless. You are Life Itself, not "a life".

Consider the metaphor of deep dreamless sleep: That questioner and all its questions disappears every time the body is laid to rest at night. There is NO difference between a body laid to rest in a bed at night and a body laid to rest in the cemetery!

In the dream at night there is the appearance of an I. Then that I might meet another I in the dream and ask, "what will happen to me when I die?" Then the body wakes. Where did that dream I go? Where did that dream questioner/question go?

Give the Podcasts at beingisknowing.blogspot.com a few really good listens. Let the I concept dissolve into its source of Birthlessness-Deathlessness.

Find the Source of question and questioner. Then such questions will make the bodymind stimulus response machine smile. Because it is blatantly obvious that when the body-life ends, NOTHING happens. You ARE. That. No Thing appearing AS Every Thing.

Stay with the obvious: YOU ARE. Being. Life IS. Existence IS. Presence IS. Awareness IS. All else is a meaningless tale, "told by an idiot, signifying nothing".

And the word is not the Real.

There is NO word for what You are.

And yet, you KNOW that You ARE..

Depression And Medication

Q: I've been enjoying your words, audio and written, on line. You mentioned that you are taking medication. I have been struggling with depression and social anxiety for over ten years now and I would love to hear about your experience with medications, and how you decided to take them and not contradict the awakening process. I'd like to try them, but don't see how they fit into the whole picture of awakening.

C: I no longer take any medication. That was a temporal event now passed. The body-mind was sick. It needed medical care. Like a car not running right, it was taken to a competent mechanic (doctor). After the condition cleared up the meds dropped away naturally, just as they came naturally. And isn't it obvious that Oneness, or Wholeness, MUST include medications? What could be excluded from Totality!??

Now: as to "deciding" to take or not take any meds, that was never in "my" control. This is seemingly a complex topic yet some deep investigation reveals the false which crumbles and the truth of your natural timeless being is revealed as simplicity itself.

Do not skip this investigation. As a philosopher, Herbert Spencer, noted: "There is a principle which is a bar against all information, which is proof against all arguments and which cannot fail to keep a man in everlasting ignorance--that principle is contempt prior to investigation". (This quote appears on the website of 'Sailor' Bob Adamson).

I suggest listening a few times to our Podcasts. Hopefully you will take up the inquiry into the false assumptions the mind cherishes (because it is those much cherished assumptions that are at the root of all suffering). To investigate in earnest and allow the me-concept to be seen for what it is, merely an assumption with NO reality in fact, cuts off the suffering by shutting down the energy given the false right at the fountainhead. Don't skip over this point.

If the condition you call social anxiety persists see a doctor! Nondual Spirituality is NOT a substitute for competent medical care. Don't be your own doctor re that, you'd have a fool for a patient. That said; please DO understand deeply that your suffering is a product of self-centered thinking. Here I make a notional distinction between a condition or some physical OR mental pain, which is the body announcing it needs some attention, and suffering, which is in the story of a self, a me, that OWNS such a state of appearances. Getting the mechanical issues addressed may allow a deeper looking. That is how it occurred for me.

While your Real Nature stands always shining, like the sun is always on, the relative appearances certainly can be dealt with in a practical fashion. Medications, if needed, are there as part of Totality. And so called "awakening" is a concept, a myth, that the self-centered ego holds out as a thing it must attain; all the while awakeness is already what's so. Being is Consciousness, as the Sun IS the light in this analogy.

Ponder: Body & world appears. To what? The notion 'this is my body' appears. To what? Thoughts appear. To what? Feelings appear. To what? Sleep appears, dreams appear, and wakefulness appears. To what? All of that is always changing, with a start, some duration, and then ... gone! The eternal Reality is unchanging, untouchable, invincible, absolute.

There is no other. There is only that. Not this not this not this. Just that. You are That.

What are you? The Eternal Reality PRIOR to Consciousness. Prior to both being and non-being. Some call that Timeless Being, or The Absolute Eternal State, yet NO concept can grasp or locate That. That has no location, no center, no properties.

You are THAT. Being, Consciousness, Life Itself, all appear IN That.

So Be It.

I Finally Got It ... NOT

Q: Charlie, I met with John Wheeler in Santa Cruz and left feeling like I finally got it... I was always it.... and I will never not be it. I feel like I'm not that clear on what I am anymore.

C: What you ARE is No Thing. Naked, Bare Presence. Get that clear first. And see that the 'word' 'presence is NOT the actual Presence. The words are intrinsically meaningless, yet they do POINT at The Real. NO "word" is what you really ARE.

Q: John had said you had a similar experience of feeling like you have it, then feeling like you lost it. I'm hoping you will get back to me on this. Thanks

C: Yes, I did have that experience, and that went on for a while... I would say owing to a certain stubbornness of "knowing" (falsely!) that there was someone to "attain something" NOT already always so, and a "someone" to gain that mythical "state of enlightenment" for "myself". Add to that a conviction (also patently FALSE) that there IS a "someday" when I will get it and never lose it. But does "someday" ever come?

That delusive sense of being an individual is where a little hard looking makes all the difference: looking to see, IS there a separate person with control over this or any other "process" that can found right here and right now? Seeing that there is no such thing breaks the attachment at the root to an entity that was never real, and collapses the support for the array of concepts that made up "the story of me and my suffering" right at the core.

Once pointed out clearly and once seen in the clear light of Naked Awareness, it's really all over for the storyteller. It is a permanent severing of the root, whether it "seems so" or not. What *seems* to be so is NOT what *IS* so.

In any event I found after the initial session with John, that owing perhaps to habit patterns in the brain over many years of believing and accepting "I am an individual" and I am NOT whole and complete, the story of "Charlie" certainly did spin up from time to time. But it could never again grip me in the same way or with the same illusory power. Because once this is seen, that's really IT on "you" and the entity must wither and die fully once the real has been seen (distinguished, if you like that term).

In my case, John patiently and compassionately pointed back always to the FACT, of Being, that undeniable wakefulness or empty presence that has always been here like a backdrop, a silent still background ON which the Big Show with its words-and images story of a me; a story which is pure fiction, appears. Despite the stubbornness of the fixation on me, the death blow had already been struck and the rest of the seeming process was just the last thrashes of the ego-me struggling to survive against the inexorable tide that carried the day in the end, as it always must. Nothing trumps the Real. To battle is futile. You may as well argue with gravity. This has already bitten you so I would only suggest, relax about it as best you can. And put a little trust into this as it just flat cannot fail. As I found out despite my best efforts to make if fail, so I could maintain an identity and survive as that entity. Despite the obvious fact that the conviction (false) that "I am the entity "me" brought such suffering! That was real ignorance which without John and Bob Adamson could very have continued to cause suffering until the body dropped dead. But there ain't no joy in "surviving". That fixation left me walking upright but really DEAD.

The point is it THAT could never be lost! You never could "lose" it. Because there IS no "it" to get OR lose! And the "person" who would either "get it OR lose it" quite simply does NOT exist.

So, seeing that what John points out is simply the FACT of your very Being, code name THAT, and THAT is absolutely REAL, inescapable and undeniable, breaks the conceptual cage that never was a fact, but merely a set of suppositions. And that all such tales of losing OR getting that which is already always Real, are merely appearances IN That and can never touch That.

Here is a refresher from John's site:

"Are you an appearance in the mind? If not, then it follows that what you are cannot be found in the mind. It is as simple as that.

In fact, your own presence (being and awareness) is clear and obvious and beyond doubt. The acknowledgment of that fact IS the knowing of it, for the being and knowing are one and the same. Pause here and simply relish the amazing point that you already are what you are seeking. The best response from here is "stop". Any further conceptualizing, thinking, "nutting it out" in the mind, etc., just brings you back to the concepts. Get the taste of the "stop". There are no dualities, doubts, questions, problems or issues in "that", which is your innate being as it is. From here, see that all thoughts, perceptions and feelings are arising spontaneously. They are not being generated by a "self center", or separate "me". In fact, there is no reference point of a "self center" except as an assumption. However, perceptions, feelings, thoughts, decisions and actions are naturally happening. There are thoughts, but no thinker, etc. From here, you are what you are, and life is a natural unfolding, without reference to a limited self notion. This is the essence of what is being pointed out. Do not miss the total simplicity (and utter profundity) of this!"

THAT says it all in far fewer words than it usually takes me!

If any questions that you sense I can address for you on the notion of "I got it" and "I lost it" (or "I COULD lose it") and it comes up to write or call me about that please feel free to do that.

And/Or: If there is any confusion or doubt left after reading the above quotation from John a few times and letting it "sink in" it would be best to take that up with John as you are now in "relationship" with him. And I don't want to add any input that may be less clear for you than John's expression.

Anyway, all the best to you my friend. I love you.

Same Old Pointers, Still Frustration

Followup to The 'Sailor' Bob Adamson Podcast...

Q: Hi Charlie: Thanks for the continuous stream of pointers, including a Podcast with 'Sailor' Bob Adamson. So here's where I seem to be stuck: the same thing is repeated over and over by many teachers. It can be summed up in one sentence: To quote Tony Parsons "So all there is, is this. There's nothing else, just this."

I've heard the same from Ramana, Poonjaji, Nisargadatta, Wei Wu Wei, "Sailor" Bob, John Wheeler, Jeff Foster, Nathan Gill, et al. It's very clear, I get it, clarity is here but clarity isn't it either, it's just more cause for frustration.

C: The mind's "understanding" of this message is a kind of cruel "booby prize". THAT which IS, That what-Is-Real … is absolutely BEYOND comprehension. Clarity is another trap that the seeker gets caught by … "Oh, 'I' see it now! "… "Oh yay, 'I' got it!" … "OH WOW 'I' am FREE!" The problem in all that is … cared to take a guess?

Right! It's that assumed identity clled "I". The assumed "personal entity", the assumption and conviction that "I" AM a contracted, limited individual. That's the only "culprit here: Memory of "me" and "other" being "true" so long as it's not directly challenged and seen as BULLSHIT!

But that "I" is JUST a pattern of energy contracted seemingly into a discrete entity that now suffers unnecessarily, and deep down everyone knows this "me" to be a FAKE. It is NOT that this is merely a belief; that may be a good pointer, however for most seekers (I am talking from experience here) that "belief" has gone so far into the backstory, the background of "tranquilized obviousness", that it is no longer a belief. It has become WHAT IS … to the Me-persona.

The conviction IS ... "I AM ME" and all else is NOT ME, and when that one arose (around age two) what came right along with it was "something IS wrong," "something is wrong with ME (victim) or THEM (aggressor). And so we start wars or manipulate others to get it to go "my way". That's what is virtually inevitable when you ARE that "I Am Separated from others and the whole, and something IS wrong". OF COURSE there will be the assumption "something is wrong". You've kicked yourself out of Paradise! Innocently, though.......

That one comes with another CONVICTION: I CAN'T. It is a body of declared limitations that happened in the mind of a two year old which was taken as TRUE and "imbedded". (After all, all the Big People said so, therefore it must be true, they MUST be right ...) and that becomes who we are for our "self", this "I" "me" ... and it is like being sentenced to Life In Prison. But this is a sentence passed on by a stupid, ignorant Judge after a sham trial where all the witnesses LIED through their damn teeth, and the Judge believed false assertions and so sentenced an innocent child to a life of suffering ... the cage of core beliefs, concepts.

What is so hard to see is that this cage is transparent and unreal and the Judge is our "self". "The fault, dear Brutus, is NOT in 'the stars'. It is in our assumed self". That's paraphrased, obviously ... but the point is, we do NOT see these concepts and declarations as concepts; we ARE that we are Separate, Broken, and CAN'T get fixed, CANNOT get whole and complete. Great weeping wailing and gnashing of teeth ensues ... until Wholeness Itself appears and says, hey, these self-imposed limits just ain't REAL!

So what we became as a self is: "I am SEPARATE, Something IS wrong with ME, and I CAN'T put Humpty Dumpty back together again."

The apparently separated you can put the entire manifestation together from those three assumed positions alone, and most people (not just seekers!) DO exactly that. The paradox of course is this assumed entity does SEEM to "do that" but that is not real either. Here, Now, there is NO doer anywhere. Nor is there any center anywhere. There is no time like this presence-awareness. There is nothing in the appearance that is true. Nor is it false. It is quite simply not REAL in the way we perceive it yet it is

ABSOLUTE REALITY AS No Thing. Everything IS and That is No Thing.

It's the water in a mirage, NOT REAL. It's the blue in the sky. NOT REAL.

A thought, which is all that "I" is, cannot attain thoughtlessness, silence, Being-Stillness. NO WAY. So what is the way out of this dilemma?

Q: So where does the "full stop" enter the picture? I can't do "full stop", or I would have stopped a long time ago.

C: That is really not true. Pause thought right now for a split-instant! It's happened many times, times where there was no identity-though. Driving a car perhaps, and noticing "I" was not there a few miles down the road as you were listening to the radio or talking to a friend. It's like the car was driving itself and there was also no driver of the driver!

Right now, pause here and read the next sentence OUT LOUD (the louder the better):

me me me me me me   me me me me me me me me   STOP!

In that instant there was no "identity" yet life continued to beat that heart and that body did not fall apart. You as what you REALLY ARE lives that body, appears AS all of those thoughts, feelings, assumptions, beliefs AND even AS the "unreal cage of concepts" that it seems the little me is sentenced to live in until death do it part!

And yet all of the appearance is BEING LIVED.

There is NO person; the person (persona) is an inauthentic mask we cover up our Nakedness with. What you are might be said to be Bare, Naked, Beingness.   What Dzogchen calls NON-Conceptual, Self-Shining, Ever-Fresh, Presence-Awareness, Just THIS and NOTHING ELSE. The words don't matter really though, because NO word can capture Your Essence as no Thing.

And the words No Thing are NOT the REAL No Thing! The REAL is Timeless, Centerless, Unlocatable, Unbounded BEING ... LIFE ITSELF. As Nisargadatta often said, "Don't refuse [stubbornly] to be what you are [Life Itself, No Thing] and stop pretending to be what you are not" [a person complaining and lamenting "I can't!"].There is no "you" YET YOU ARE and THAT is Life Itself. One Essence of No Thing APPEARING as EVERYTHING and EVERYONE....

Q: The search goes on, it's insatiable. The answer is always around the next bend. I'm old, tired and frankly, sick of the game. Again, Tony Parsons: "it goes on until it doesn't". I guess I've just answered my own question, never mind, thanks for listening.

C: All these "nondual concepts" are absolutely useless when believed, accepted, known. Knowing all that stuff and parroting some friend's concepts is to turn the direct immediacy of THAT which is REAL into a bunch of beliefs. It is to turn Nonduality into a new religion with it's collection of dogmatic convictions and it is all just bullshit. ALL words are bullshit. ALL of them!

Reality is NOT a word, and no statement can grasp REALITY. You are NOT a word, NOT a thing. You are No Thing AKA Life Itself.

Now STOP. LOOK. Listen ... lest this runaway train keep running you into the ground over and over.

BE as You are: No Thing. Everything. LIFE-Livingness, Energy. Nothing but THAT.

Life IS. Absolute Being. Only THAT. The "relative" is the Absolute pretending to be two, ten, ten million, many, all. The Ten Zillion Things are all YOU. Isn't that a trip!?

Give Bob's Podcast a few more listens ... each "time" from a space of NOT Knowing anything, discarding everything anyone has ever said, being open and empty. STOP LISTEN LOOK. Then seeing rightly can happen in the Instant. The identity falls through the net of concepts in a free-falling out-of-control-ness beyond all knowing and not knowing. Being Life Itself brings effortless living and the natural "playing out" of the character's "time here" in absolute freedom and causeless joy.

Thank you for writing. I Love You.

Follow-up

Q: Thank you Charlie, for taking the time to answer my lament with so much depth and love. I can only say - I love you back.

C: Yep... That's all that's left when there is only That which you are in Reality... I Love You. "When I don't know who I am, I love You. When I know who I am, I AM You." Good job!

"Things are not what the seem to be. Nor are they otherwise."

Is This Just More Story?

Q: I just wanted to share something with you. Last night, I had difficulty falling asleep, it's as if thoughts were coming fast and furious and there was a watching of them. But this went on for hours, and I could feel a contraction in my chest/abdomen area as it happened. So is this just more story? There seems to be a genuine unfolding here, but I really don't know how to interpret it, perhaps I shouldn't even try. Ok, honestly, my question doesn't make much sense anymore, but I'll post it anyways since I already typed it up. Thanks for reading it.

C: I enjoyed this! So, THAT is what happened (apparently!) in the Waking Dream called "this life".

There can certainly seem to be an unfolding (or maybe more accurately a "collapsing" of the illusion of 'me') ... anything is possible as Oneness rediscovers Itself and the little individual fades away and than BANG! Dead and Gone yet Life is still living that body, mind, being absolute freedom (relatively speaking!)

That sense of contraction has been there since around the age of two, but covered over by the mask (persona) which is just a "cage of concepts" which forms what some call an "energetic contraction".

ALL words are ALWAYS "story' but once the false entity collapses and dies then LIFE ITSELF, the infinite Intelligence-Energy that is No thing appearing as EVERYTHING, tells the story in freedom and joy. The PLAY goes on but the "player" is no more. The realization is that there is only ever Wholeness, and that INCLUDES both the "contraction" AND the "re-expansion" out of contraction back into Timeless Being-Reality.

Just be clear that NO one can "do" anything about this. (There IS no one like a person to do or undo anything!) We sometimes discuss "investigation" or "looking for the entity" but NO one is in control of that or any other apparent process! Ultimately the perfect way to avoid "liberation" is to SEEK it.

Yet anything can appear. Anything is possible. It may even be that the great Heart of ruthless LOVE may "infect" the brain with a virus that utterly destroys the belief-feeling "I AM ME". NO ONE IS IN CHARGE ANYWHERE! There IS the "killer of illusion" Everywhere! And Nowhere!

In FACT: It is ALL Just Happening! Being IS and occurs to be separate and occurs to end its separateness! And no "one" can "cause" that ... why? An illusion cannot dispel illusion!

There IS no 'separate one'! There is ONLY Being. The ONLY Reality is Being. Being is REAL and your authentic Beingness IS THAT. Being IS and no one can deny or escape from THAT.

You are THAT. And THAT is LOVE.

Q: Thanks so much for your answer, especially the last four lines. Ok so I knew this already. And I noticed that when I asked the question to begin with, there was a sense of loss of power, as if I was needing validation, I was seeking clarity again, when all there ever is, is clarity. Oh well, the story continues, sometimes in clarity, sometimes not so much, but I'm finding it harder and harder to care about this. I mean if I'm all it, and that's what it feels like now, then what do I really care what's happening to the "little character", I mean I do care, but I also don't care, you know what I mean?

C: This cannot be "known. This is not "knowledge" and not ignorance either. All those concepts are irrelevant. The real is the know-ING.

There is NO I. That I-word is a JUST another fictitious concept.

So who cares?

When there is no longer the addiction to "being me" then it is seen that THIS is all there is, and THIS is just an appearance in THAT... That Being-Wholeness. So even "separation is Wholeness playing at the Game Called Life. Dramatic comedic move, this...

You are dreaming, my friend. And the dreamed can NEVER "wake himself or herself".

THAT ... Being-Wholeness ... both Is and Is Not. As Bob Adamson has said, it is not seen and it is seen. Let that sit there, let it steep.

If there is a belief in some being teachers and others being seekers, then that very belief is the mind's ignorance. Given that paradigm, I/other, the seeking will go on absolutely of its own energy (the same energy that beats that heart and patterns as all these bodyminds and all the stars and universes) and there really is NO HOPE of "attaining" anything because there just AIN'T NO PERSON in there. That is seen or not, but the seeing of this or not has nothing to do with the FACT of Being.

Ask yourself this: Can space know it is space? Can emptiness "know" emptiness? Can the Self (No Thing) KNOW it is no thing? The subject-object ideation-contraction IS the ignorance of mind. YOU cannot ever get it. YOU in Reality ARE it. IT is NOT an appearance, IT is NO Thing.

Bottom line: You are No Thing. And No thing cannot "attain" no thing.

What IS "I"? A thought. Can a thought see? Seeing is always ALREADY happening. "Trying to see with the mind, the "I', is a fools errand. IT IS TRULY HOPELESS.

Thoughts come and go IN the seeing Itself. That is NOT a concept, NOT a state, NOT a feeling. It is NO THING.

YOU are THAT. No thing but No thing is all.

It's all just happening as it IS... beyond control, the Great River Of Life Itself, taking "you" home, Killing you softly with Ruthless love!

That is Love. Formless Being-Knowing.

Love Is That. Nonconceptual Love, beyond comprehension or description.

Tat Tvam Asi. That Thou Art.

224

Inaccurate Interpretations of What Is

Q: Listening to what we talked about [in a one on one consultation] I felt like saying that the feeling of something missing in life is not actually a question of something missing, but actually a bad interpretation of something falsely present. namely, the false me which filters and distorts what's there. the me is what makes the picture look incomplete. (to me). and if we look around, at all those apparent people walking and not having any idea of the problematic ME, it may be seen that the picture is full and complete as it is. but not for 'me'.

C: Okay...

Q: I just realized tonight something I have felt vaguely for a long time but couldn't put into words. and that is that the enjoyment of watching movies is partly because they are just stories in which I am not there.

I don't know if that makes any sense but there is clarity about it here. thank you.

C: Good insight. now watch the movie "you" are the star in and realize you ain't there in THAT move show either!

Q: That is what is being longed for Charlie

C: It is already the case. Read this over:

This message is incredibly powerful and freeing when it's taken on as YOU speaking to YOU rather than listening as though there are two personas yakking at each other. That's all machinery and only YOU (Your SELF, not the persona) can bring about the Full Stop. Otherwise you'll get great experiences that come and go leaving you "weeping and wailing and gnashing your teeth!" Been there done that no joy in that bullcrap....

To paraphrase the philosopher Ludwig Wittgenstein: The words on these pages serve as pointers, as propositions that serve as elucidations in the following way: anyone who "understands" these words must transcend these propositions, to stand upon them and look out from atop them like standing on a ladder or platform raised above the landscape of the sleepwalking obvious everydayness, then step OFF of and away from the platform, throw out the ladder, step out in a kind of free-fall of NOT KNOWING...and then the world may be seen rightly as what-it-is ... No Thing in Essence, Every Thing in appearance, the Grand Hologram. In finality, THIS can NOT be "languaged" as language is a domain of division, distinction and separating this from that. So finally, as Wittgenstein said, "Whereof one cannot speak, thereof one must be SILENT."

Understanding 'nonduality' is the BOOBY PRIZE...... !!

In UNKnowing-Being there is ONLY the Great Silence appearing as BEING-KNOWINGNESS ... Silence Banging the doors and yelling I LOVE YOU ... noises on and noises off. IN This Silence is the absolute absence of presence and the absence of absence. Incomprehensible Reality, clear and always this Forever-Moment, ON never OFF, and right HERE before all that appears IN it. Silently Being, Obviously Knowing, yet NOT "knowing of or by a me".... OKAY?

You are already whole and complete. This is NOT a pipe dream. Not an "attainment". It is a FACT, the actual Reality of YOUR True Nature. I'll show you this; you can get this and BE the freedom you are, if you are willing to be open to giving up what you know for just a few minutes. That's your part of the bargain, to put to rest once and for all this notion that "something is wrong, I am suffering and trying to attain freedom, I am not good enough" or any (and all) of the other self-invented lies we tell ourselves in our ignorance.

I say, You are whole and complete. For now let us take this as an assertion. If you understand "legal language", then you know that an assertion is a particular kind of speaking in which the commitment is to provide evidence to back up why you claim something to be true.

So if you are interested in getting at what is REAL, then you would be asking, "Okay, YOU say I am whole and complete. But

HOW do you know that? What is the evidence?" Fair enough! So now watch:

Is it possible for you to have "being NOT whole and complete"? Can you really start out from Not something"? Isn't it true that to have NOT something, to have NOT whole and complete, there MUST FIRST BE the "condition" called IS whole and complete? There just can't be IS NOT without IS! You cannot be NOT a condition, the actual condition Wholeness" MUST be there to have "Not wholeness".

So: You may not be experiencing "whole and complete" right now but that is an experience happening in the context of, the SPACE of, I AM whole and complete. So it is simply NOT possible to NOT be whole and complete without it's opposite, I AM whole and complete. In the world of relative livingness every position also contains its opposite position. But let's move beyond the relative now and get at this from another perspective.... namely the perspective of Being No Thing.

Let's move from asserting a thing to be true or false to declaring a thing to be SO regardless of apparent contrary evidence.

A Declaration is a kind of speaking for which the declarer, the speaker, is solely responsible, and there is no time frame or deadline -- yet. There may be a time line spoken but it is not an essential element. It may be specific, but there's no time involved. Declarations are outside of "time". And require NO "proof". The word stands by itself, on it's own. Declarations are neither true nor not true; true and not true appear in a DIFFERENT domain of speaking and listening; in the domain of presence, of assertions with evidence. Declarations are speech ACTS IN the domain of BEING. What is present, what is conceptualized, what is experienced, and even your "idea of being me" occurs (or is asserted) IN the domain of BEING.

To get at this for yourself, I'd like you to consider the white space all around the letters, these symbols, to be like the Space that you really ARE; the Space of Being No Thing. Then notice that as that SPACE, you are neither complete NOR incomplete.

Those stories are some CONTENT appearing IN the Space and do not alter or affect the space. Are you with me?

Now here is where this gets difficult. Here is where we produce, from our Self, a different domain for language, namely as noted above, the Timeless domain of Being . But Being-As-WORD. Word, as a declaration, rather than an assertion. What do I mean? I mean that when you ... YOU ... DECLARE I Am Whole and complete as a context, then the content of I am or I am not is simply some irrelevant noises appearing in the CONTEXT YOU create. It is a kind of "sacred saying", I AM whole, I AM complete, and when that is the space YOU create and stand in and for, then you are no longer a leaf on the wind, no longer a little petty complaining entity but rather life is happening in the space that you are. This is real FREEDOM, and authentic POWER, the power of BEING, BEING your word (as in the powerful saying "in the beginning IS the Word"; not the sounds or squiggles of everyday conversation in your head or "out there" but Word like No Thing, Being What IS.

You become, actually, You ARE, the source of what you are, what you do and what appears in this space. Not like this is TRUE. You make it YOUR truth, because you say so. You return your Self to the Home you never actually left.

It's really simple so give up the attempt to "figure this out" as best you can. It is this simple: You stand on your own two feet, with NO props, and NO proof, and you DECLARE, I am Whole and Complete. If you want to assign "cause" then that goes like this: I am whole and complete BECAUSE I am whole and complete. Not to be right about it! NO. To simply STAND in No Thing and declare that as a context for your life and for life itself. Then (NOW) YOU ARE Life Itself. This is a kind if Silent Knowing, like Being-Knowing. You can't prove or disprove it; that would be an assertion. YOU ARE IT.

Why? You are Whole "because" you are Whole. In the same way the Wright brothers said, man can fly, like a declared possibility, and could live into the lack of the fact of it, into the "consensus reality" best expressed as "If God had meant for man to fly He would have given him wings", into that resigned cynicism, Orville and Wilbur stood OUTSIDE "creation" and DECLARED. From where? From nowhere. From Everywhere. From The Self.

Got it? Well, this is something that cannot be known and real unless YOU create it. No one can "give you" being. It is really up to you. Don't try to "understand" this. Understanding at this level is the booby prize. You must INVENT this for your Self.

Whack! The ball is now in YOUR court. I Love You. (Why? Because I Love You).

Q: Yes. thank you. it is like that. Yet climbing and jumping off the ladder doesn't seem like something I can do. Any effort here meets frustration. however, I can see that it is the me that says that and put the bars to its own prison, but I suppose that's going to keep happening until it doesn't. in the end I don't have a flying clue.

C: You need to read that a lot more deeply. Give up trying to "get this with the mind", and really GO DEEP. You cannot create from something. First you must COMMIT to BE NO THING (since THAT is what is REAL.)

"Argue for your limitations, and sure enough, they're yours!"

~ Richard Bach, "Illusions"

Awareness Is Not "Covered Over By Mind"

Q: The mind is still very active; however awareness is not covered by it.

C: BINGO! Once that clicks, that signals the end of seeking. Also: There is nothing "wrong" with thinking, and feeling; that's ALIVENESS happening in the Space and always you are Being the Space IN which all this appears, comes and goes, plays and dies. It's clear in what you write (here and before) that THIS is obviously what's so, the Reality there now.

Good seeing!

Now what may not be completely clear in our experiencing the Isness of Life happening is you and I are ALSO that "content in the Space". As has been pointed out in ten thousand awesome ways, the space and the content of the space are Not Two.

Q: Much love.

C: Back Atcha!

Knowing The Self Is A Firm Conviction

Q: Hi Charlie, saw your web TV interview with Richard on nevernothere.com. Loved it.

C: That was FUN ... especially the chats with those who called in.

Q: I have visited with Sailor Bob in Melbourne and have had a number of correspondences with John Wheeler. Re-cognised the natural state of cognizing emptiness when with Bob. Still identified with the contractions of dualistic conceptions much of the time though overall I have been living life as a waking dream for about 15 years.

C: Is that really true? Or are you simply buying a lie and making it real by your own repeated declaration? It's worth looking at! When I was at Bob's place, it all seemed clear and obvious. But later I realized that the idea that I got that from BOB is a big fat lie! As Bob himself is always pointing out, there is nothing that any "other" can give "another" for there just IS no "other" ... unless YOU say there is, in the mind or language.

Being separated, being a me that is "still identified" with the "contracted me" is a matter of YOU lying to yourself and believing that lie! Realize that YOU are the only one who can limit you, and you do so in languaging a separate "self" AND by inventing a thing called time, as in "I still" which supposes a past that is actually long gone. The LIE also provides a future you live into which is ALWAYS a product of the past until you break through that by being willing to actually BE what YOU ACTUALLY ARE ... No Thing, living AS which, ANYTHING is possible.

What you are IS pure possibility, however hearing that makes NO difference unless YOU create that, stand for THAT as an existential act of courage and love. You stand nowhere and declare I am NOT a thing, I AM No Thing. And all contrary positions are false. As is said so often, the ball finally is in your court. Bob once said to me, "you gotta stand on your own two feet" regarding completing, and sharing about, the search.

As Sri Nisargadatta declared (DECLARED, not asserted), "I take my stand where no difference exists, where things are not, nor the minds that create them. There I am at home." What makes you think you are really any different from Maharaj, or Bob? Find out!

Q: What's your take on the process of identification? 'I' have lived in the absence of the person on about 10 occasions from about 5 seconds to about 20 hours clock time but sooner or later turned it into experience and thus memory ... ad nauseam. Suggestion?

C: Always, experience (presence-experiencing) devolves to concept (memory). That's just the way we're built! To have your focus on circumstances (presence, concept) is to trap yourself by taking some experiences-memories to be more valid or special than others. But ALL experience passes in this Instant-Before-Time; every "thing, whether the thing be memory of a happening or the presence of experiencing some state, all leaves as soon as it arises so to try to grab onto such an ephemerality (my word) is to go utterly astray!

In fact there is actually (ACTUALLY) NO "process of identification! That is just another "likely story" that the asserted self-called-me tells itself as a way to avoid confronting its own absolute meaninglessness and emptiness!

Q: Life in the waking dream .... Wonderful mystery!

C: There is NO mystery when you have your stand in no thing. You simply ARE ... Being. Being No Thing. Because why? Because nothing, no "reason". Reasons are in the domain of the falsely asserted "me". Standing nowhere takes a kind of existential courage; the courage to BE as you really are. And that is a stand only YOU can create.

Q: Thanks again for the sharing.

C: It's a privilege and a deep pleasure, communicating this, like Bob says, "From I Am to I Am!" Thank YOU for writing. The invitation is open, the secret is out; you are that Self of All. To paraphrase a text from the nondual expression called Kashmir

Shaivism, Knowing Thy Self is a FIRM CONVICTION. It's a matter of giving up the lies in favor of the reality, and therein suffering is no more (and never was nor could ever be.)

Write again if you like. Meanwhile KNOW THIS. You ARE Love.

Nothing Is Not Oneness

A correspondent writes, "Hey Charlie, I really liked reading about those conflicts with [a 'teacher' who shall remain unmanned here], as they show a side to this nonduality stuff that is often overlooked. I've heard you say that the seeing of oneness isn't some sort of "fix" for the character in the appearance, or something similar to that. "Dark spots in the mind" and reacting to content and what not still seem to go on... for no one. The only difference I see is that the suffering of pretending to be a person amplifies and personalizes all these happenings. There is a greater capacity for forgiveness when it is seen that there is no real doer of any deed, no real actor of any action.

If I am a "me", I will see threatening and undesirable people "out there." If I am Being itself, there are only characters appearing in what I am, as I appear as a character to the apparent other.

C: YES! That is IT in a nutshell.

Q: The love you speak of is palpable and more real than any of the content, and to me that is the message. I have never been able to love anyone until this message began to hit home, so I thank you once again my friend. Much love, M.

C: Very beautifully and eloquently said. Thank YOU, my very dear friend!

A Review Of The Basics Of It

1. YOU are Awareness, simply being. No one can say they do not exist. That existence, the sense of "I" as in "I Am," is undeniable and inescapable. Try to NOT BE. Cannot be done. So the simple pointer is, what you are is That Presence or Awareness. That, YOU ARE. Being. Just That! This True You ... BE-ING... is POINTED TO in language with concepts like Impersonal Consciousness; God, Peace, Self, I AM, Awareness, Life, Bliss, Existence, Being ... YOU are just THAT, prior to the mind's translation into the thought I Am and I am this or that.

2. You are NOT an "individual." There are NO "individuals" anywhere except in unreal stories. The idea of a separate person is a fiction, a mind-construction, a house of cards, as the story tries to say, "I'm ME! (Unsuccessfully!) This idea of a "me" is ... on investigation ... seen to be a false claim by the thinking machinery to it's own separate existence. This ever-changing idea of a person is simply unreal. WHO says "I'm Me?" The mind. To be blunt, it's bullshit. The whole fabricated story of me is pure bullshit: all stories of "individuals" is actually a fiction. As Shakespeare said, it's a tale told by an idiot, filled with sound and fury, signifying ... NOTHING.

Look right now! Seeing with naked Awareness, where is any person ... unless you (as a mind-identity) think about it? Thoughts come and go. What you ARE NEVER comes and goes anywhere. It is (You Are) fully Here Now and Eternally Free and Clear, Eternally Presence, Shining before the mind.

YOU are not a thought, not a concept, not a feeling, not a time bound entity. You are Awakeness, Aliveness, Presence-Awareness. Just THAT and NOTHING else. The story of "me" ... ANY "me" ... is irrelevant. Let's cut through that crap right now! Okay?

Let's bring this back to the basics: What in YOU never changes? Being-Awareness, just That. That is your True Nature. Where is a separate entity when you are in deep dreamless sleep? Or under anesthesia? There is none. Obviously! But some Presence beats the heart, breathes air in and out, flows the blood, grows new cells and disintegrates other cells, grows hair and fingernails, ages the body etc etc! Who or what is "doing" all that? Not an individual, "one who is "special", "amazing" "ordinary" or any label. No labels apply.

Look and see that you are present and aware right now. That is the "Eternal," The Natural State; there is no other, no attainment, no flashy enlightened state, no carrot on a stick. There is NO someday when "you" will "get enlightened." It's what you are right now. There is no other than NOW. Wherever you are, you ARE ... Here. That's IT. Big Casino.

You've already got it in total (because you ARE IT) and there's nothing more to this Nonduality stuff than that simple seeing, that you ARE fully present Awareness, Simply That. Period. Full Stop.

In our meeting and conference calls, there's just friends, sharing what works to end any suffering and recognize (directly, immediately and naturally) that you are already free and clear.

There's nothing to get and no one to get it. Drop the belief in "individuality" and there you are, Present and Alive, the Light of loving being, just that, nothing else. That's IT.

There's No hidden meanings, no secret, no special persons, no teachings ... just what already always IS.

Suchness.

Just SO.

Afterparty At The Masquerade Ball

There are more than six billion dancers at the Masquerade Ball tonight.

Six billion masks, hiding scared insecure children. Called "me".

Some are wielding weapns of mass destruction.

Some are wielding flowers and an olive branch.

Some are wielding bibles to ward off evil.

Some are wielding evil to ward off bibles.

Some are dressed up as robbers, murderes, and rapsits.

Some are dressed up as police, prosecutors, judges, juries and jailers.

Some are garbed as saints, and some are clothed as sinners.

Some are hiding in a suit of armor and some are hiding in a suit of nakedness, hunger and disease. Famine. Despair

And some are seen to be sitting high and mighty, pretending to spout their version of wisdom-truth from their mountain-top or or their Tall Chair on the Big Stage, always pretending to be special and obviously superior to those clothed as seekers of truth who grovel and beg for a scrap of attention and a glance from the Master On High.

All the dancers dance to One Tune, One Energy, One Essence, One Love appearing as love/hate, good/evil, powerful /powerlessness, man/woman, living/dying.

And all are secretly terrified that their mask may slip and there will be nakedness, the Unmasked Isness, alone yet all One.

All are secretly afraid of falling in love with what is. They hang on to limits for a dear life which is far from dear.

And a very very few like YOU dear reader may pray that the mask be melted in the fire of Love/Compassion ... just NOW. Right Now.

Thsoe nonentities whose masks have melted (despite all their best efforts at prevention) are saying, "Hey there? Your mask is making you suffer and there is no need for that."

But since those appearances wear NO mask, thus they are unheard by the born ones. The unmasked, being Unborn, cannot be perceived by the hapless apparemtly born idenitty.

Never. So Sorry. The Masquerade Ball has its own rules!

The Mask has made them deaf, dumb, and blind, kid. (And some play a mean pinball!)

"Rip off the mask! The Ball is ending!", the phantom unmasked shouts to the upright dead who have ears they own, and so cannot hear. Only one with no ears hears and heeds the Unmaked One who is "heard-by-no-one."

But the Guru dancer, the dream dancer who exhorts and urges, never realizes that He/She is sporting the most opaque mask of all. The mask of Wise Man. Enlightened Woman. Knower Of The Truth.

Yet those who claim to "know it", knows it NOT; the mask talks and the naked hide behind that. The Emperor is naked; he has NO clothes on. And believes the mirrior mirror on the wall, the "me" who all dressed up as fairest of them all! Atempt to point out his nakedness and it will be "Off with your head, you bloody infidel!"

(Ummm ... THAT is not a half bad idea, actually.)

O masked ones like me: We who invent endless futile practices and studies of "God" etc: Can we not see? "Oh say can we see? By the Dawn's early Light?"

That No One masks themselves as someones?

The mask was applied by The Forever Unmasked One Him-Her-It-Self ... the timeless genderless IS. Call That Awareness, call That Being, or just call That ... THAT.

THAT masks itself, dresses up for a long night of dancing ... why? Just for the hell of it. Just for the heaven of it.

Let's call THAT "divine Mother". (Why not? Any name for the infinite Nameless is as good or bad as any other...)

I Am ... the Mother ... masks Her Self with the billions of masks of selves ... so She can dance with Her Self! Why NOT?

She masks Her Self and dances with no-one-but-her-Self in Her trillion trillion galaxies, universes, blades of grass and dead stars, supernovas and a baby born this moment. She. Is. All. She Is. Is YOU.

The Real Unmasked You. Hello, I love you, won't you tell me your Name?

She plays the unwritten parts of God and Devil with glee and mourning, joy and sadness, sure looks lie ... being born and dying over and over and over ... but She (YOU) forever Remain Unborn...

And every "now and then" "here and there" She unmasks Time Itself and winks at Her reflection in her mirror ... the small you ... and smiles with the Radiance of Ten Thousand Suns and the 'you' mask melts and ahhhhhhh "I Am That" ... NOW it is clear ... empty ... filled ... just Love and Nothing Else IS... Now. And Now. And Now.

Tears of joy well from deep within and appear Here as the freshness of the spring rainfall as She renews Herself again and again and again but always only NOW...

So plain to see that the masks could never have neen removed by the one wearing it; only by the One who "created" the mask..... and then forgot so as to be entranced, enthralled ... for the wow if it, the lovestory and horror movie... called This Life.....

The Silent Goddess of the Deep Black Night who gently steals the Her persona of ignorance away ... to kiss the lips of her Self, to reunite what was never separate.

Being, Unborn.

Appearing as you and me and life itself.

Jsut for the Love of it all!

And so the Masquerade Ball goes on and on

And She is unmasking her Self Just Now.

Here.

Let Her. If you can.

This is Living Oneness. Awake and Alive in Timeless Peace.

Being Unborn, Being Life Itself.

You Are Unborn.

You Are Life Itself.

If You Would Like To Talk About This:

This direct message is a sharing, not a teaching as such. And it is very, very simple. No long retreats are offered here (nor any "short retreats for that matter"). The direct seeing and knowing that frees the seeker from suffering and seeking for some imagined state to be attained in some also imagined "future" undercuts the need for protracted "practices or processes". Here, there were a few direct talks with Bob Adamson, and John Wheeler. No "decades-long" process was ever required, as some deluded "teachers" claim! Only an openness to "hear with no ears", to listen with an open mind and heart.

This simple message requires no "preparation", no "ripeness", no special reading or study, no daily "resting in awareness", and no particular "smarts", to imbibe.

Make no mistake; it IS possible to live (or more accurately, BE Lived) in Freedom, and the Natural Stateless State of true Peace; loving what is, as it is.

Feel free to write to non.duality@yahoo.com with any brief questions; and please be aware that your e-mail "q and a" may be published for the benefit of other seekers who visit here. But for a more direct approach, get in touch. Call +1 580 701-4793 any time and leave a message or write me an e-mail.

We suggest a $70 donation for each "formal" consultationm (usually 60 to 90 minutes). If you cannot afford that we are open to receiving whatever you can afford. Usually two or three of these sessions are all that is needed, providing you are willing to "Stop, Look, and Listen!" Meanwhile, no that the truth of who you are lies in the direct knowing of That which is Aware of you own sense of Being ... I AM". As has been shared over millennia, THAT, Thou Art. Period; Full Stop.

Feel free to get in touch with any questions or comments, or to request a One to One meeting by Phone, in perosn, or on Skype.

You can reach me most days between 10 AM and 6 PM USA Central Time (GMT -6 Hours).

What is Possible ...

From 'being different' to Being Reality ... the end of seeking and the dissolution of the "myth of enlightenment"

Q: I have been watching some of your clips on YouTube and reading some on your blog. And I have a question: A couple of months ago "I" had this experience of how my true identity was not me as a person. There was just this nothingness and the one I thought was me was just seen as an illusory identity. Like a software program in this mind/body-mechanism to make it able to function in this physical dimension. But this mechanism had no identity, because, well, it's just a mechanism. Instead there was NO me at all. NO identity. Or you could also say that "my" identity was a vast nothingness. I'm not really a person.

C: Exactly. That is the core insight... the seeing-knowing that yes, there is no person, and that seeing IS the timeless reaity. Now, however, you say "there WAS no person". There still IS no person, and there never was or could be a real separate "person"; that was and is only a false assumption taken on board as an identity that never was more than a mirage, an illusion. But that is ONLY a concept and NO concept is "true"!

Moreover, the idea "there WAS no person' is just presently arising thought in unchanging naked awareness. You ARE that Naked Awareness. No idea or concept is the Real You. Even to say "You are Naked Awareness" is in a way, false; or only a pointer. The word is NOT the actual.

Q: And to come to my question; after this it has been problematic to find the so called "meaning" with anything. Somehow I can't see the point in anything. Meaning with life? ... I can't see any such thing. So what if someone becomes "realized", "enlightened" or whatever? (I don't see how anyone can BECOME something because it seems we are just eternal awareness/consciousness anyway.).

C: Quite right, my friend. But remember that the concept awareness/consciousness is not the actual space-like essence at all. NO word can capture what is essentially wordless, yet paradoxically, filled with energy and a very alive presence. "Form is emptiness, emptiness is form" is a good pointer: These are NOT TWO. This is Non-Duality.

Q: The concept of "meaning" just doesn't stick to anything anymore. This nothingness seems to be "stuck" in every aspect of my life.

C: Whose life!? This is a reinforcement of the false … the return of an assumption held onto that there actually IS a "person" … and now that "person" claims "there is no person". That's why the pointer "there is no person" really does not get at what we need to get at … the assumption itself, the preverbal "knowing I am me" that is still operating here. Your sharing shows that this false assumption is still operating "in deep background' and it is that which needs to be challenged, uprooted, and found to be unreal.

Q: Suddenly everything is nothing. Even emotions. My emotions seem almost numb somehow. Everything is no neural and in a way very dull.

C: Yes, that can happen so long as that assumption referenced above remains fundamentally and directly unchallenged.

As John Wheeler reminded me repeatedly "Understanding is the key." Understanding comes form investigation. Get really curious to see what this I is that claims "there's no meaning" or "it's all empty and numb somehow". That is "the end game". Get down to brass tacks: what IS this assumed sense of life, sense of being, that still operates as a seemingly separate me-person despite the insight that happened. Yesterday's insight has no value at all; it's dead conceptualizing now. Presently, what is real? Your Being Itself. That Being remains forever, Unborn. No thing yet appearing as everything. To paraphrase Sri Nisargadatta, when the seeing "I am no one" happens there arises wisdom. Bit that is only half of this. When the seeing is I am everything, that is Love. And this love is the Reality of your very Being. Which Nisargadatta expressed as, "My silence sings. My emptiness is full". So the invitation is to get very very interested in what it is that "feels numb: and asserts "there is no one". If there is truly no one who would be making these claims of some lack or limitation, some apparent suffering? The false cannot stand up to solid, earnest investigation. The ball is in your court now my friend. Please feel free to write again as the One moves that to arise and happen. Meanwhile, BE. Just BE what you already ARE, Naked Unborn Awareness ... and only That. Seeing into the manifestation with and from naked Awareness, find out of that assumed sense-of-me is real once and for all. Thanks for a good question. Cheers and love,

Q: Thanks a lot Charlie for your very in-depth answer. You have no idea how much this means to me.... or maybe you have some idea. Anyway, I have some contemplation to do now.

C: It's my pleasure! Stay in touch. Let's nail this down once and for good.

Q: There still seems to exist a duality in "me". Even though that duality can't be real. On the one hand, the person is not there and instead there is nothing, a vast vacuum or space or eternal sea where no ripple can be created. Focusing on that is blissful.

C: Well perhaps but that is a pendulum swing and the other side of it is suffering! Blissful states are temporary. All states are temporary and NOT what we are pointing to as your True Self!

Q: I like that expression, "Eternal Sea where no ripple can be created".

C: That's really not all that clear. The ripples are the same essence of water as the sea: This is NOT TWO. In the same way that your essence of pure Awareness and all the seemingly separate appearances are ALL that same essence. Not Two.

Q: And on the other hand it is not being understood or seen how this space, nothingness or whatever is also everything. "Form is emptiness and emptiness is form". That doesn't quite compute here for some reason. The nothingness is more like. Well, just simply nothing, and not even nothing because nothing is just a word. How the everything is the same as that, or one with it, is not seen.

C: Can there be two no things? Oneness IS No Thing NOT Two... Also, "everything" is also just a word, a concept. NO concept can ever capture or define what you are! The No Thing is NOT a thing that the mind can grasp or own; Awareness, No Thing, is NOT personal and NOT an object with properties. It appears that there is still a subtle fixation on being "someone" who is somehow defective because "it is not being understood". Do you need to understand this to BE? Awareness is absolutely no thing and that means NO thing. Yet is, that No Thing, is infused with Freedom and Aliveness; we call that Aliveness ... Simple Being! Life Being Life. Your Real Self.

Please start out from the one FACT you cannot escape or deny: You ARE. Being IS! Irrefutable. Or Awareness IS. That true nature is never not here and never touched by any concept or object. But to make "no thing" into an object will also lead to making "everything" into ANOTHER separate object. This will keep the tacitly assumed self-center (the pre-verbal "I AM the me" assumption) in place and keep the mind spinning in this confusion. But the idea of being someone is ONLY a passing fancy and a learned notion adopted by a two-year-old's brain and imbedded and it kind of has turned solid. But it is NOT actually solid when looked directly into. This is why investigation must happen to root out the false assumption that "there IS a 'me' and that 'me' IS real". It's a belief and NOT what actually IS. It takes discrimination and looking, rather than stopping at some assertion like "I am no thing" because that statement will just become another definition pasted onto your true indefinable nature.

Q: But is there really a need for that understanding? I mean, who is trying to understand it?

C: What is needed is the understanding of A) what you ARE and B) the mechanics of suffering and assumed separation. That's is essential. That's what is shared here.

Q: And I notice how I put that in the terms of "on the one hand...and on the other hand", like there are two separate things when in fact there is not. But still that understanding is not being felt and understood here... or is that just the fake person sneaking up from the shadows like a zombie creating a kind of separation?

C: No explanation will satisfy because what wants an explanation is a false self that has no more real existence than Santa Claus. And who is this "I" that says "I notice?" "I put..." etc? Where is it? What is that I-assumption, that self-center, actually made of? Presently arising thoughts, appearing in the empty space of your true nature of Awareness.

The crucial point is that the culprit is that an intrinsically meaningless I-thought being given an "assumed reality". It is a kind of spiritual immaturity; like still believing is Santa Claus who once the child is a few years older is seen to be a totally false assumption. This is no different! See through this by looking in at the mind's chatter from your natural timeless state of aware presence. That is never missing and there is never anything wrong in and as That. Abide as That and LOOK...

Shine the natural light of that naked "I AM" Awareness on the false belief. It's like sneaking downstairs and seeing that there is no Santa Claus; seeing daddy putting the presents out under the tree, and mommy drinking the mike you left out, and eating the cookies... where in the past you took the presents and the remaining crumbs and empty milk glass as your "proof" of the existence of Santa.

Also, take NO identification on board, EVEN an identity called "I am no thing" OR I am everything. And look at this from another angle now:

Seeking "Wholeness, Completion, Happiness, Love or "Liberation" from "Another", whether that "revered other" be a "Guru, Guide, Lover, or Friend", is a perfect way to avoid Paradise. Paradise is THIS. Just as it Is and just as it Isn't.

All seeking "out there" is a dream of a "me", foolishly knocking on the door to Paradise, from inside Paradise. Paradise is only lost in seeking it. This Loving Oneness Cannot Be Known.

To "know" Oneness there would have to be a sense of separation FROM Oneness. Who cannot see the fault in that logic?

WHO assumes there is a defective "me" that lacks some understanding? Ask this until the falseness of that assumption is seen clearly: What IS this "I" or "me" that "wants to understand and/or experience itself as being everything?" Where is that thing? IS that a thing, with a beginning, middle and end? Find out; see for yourself, that the ignorance-assumption of separateness, of a "me", is merely a thought-assumption construct made of air. What is that "thing" that wants more than naked awareness? That true self is freedom itself. WHO wants more than freedom?

Bottom line is YOU are NOT a thing and yet Awareness ... Being-Aliveness ... your True Nature ... IS. Always. Just. So.

And, the "I" is a word that refers to ... what? Nothing! Non-Objective Being, appearing as the Consciousness-Presence, conceptualized as "I AM" But YOU are That which is PRIOR TO that "I AM" concept and even prior to the Consciousness-Knowingness Itself! YOU are Pure Being that does not know that it is. THIS is Nonduality... One-No-Other.

Your actual NON-conceptual Being is not an object with properties therefore It cannot be attained, described or defined. See that clearly right now and the search is done.

Q: Wow...Thanks so much for all this. I have never spoken to anyone who have ever been able to help like this and provide answers or pointers like this to the kind of questions that are appearing from this apparent person called Björn. Basically, everyone would think that I'm just getting crazy (if I told them about it). But it seems on the contrary to be very sane. Or actually.. there is no one thinking I am getting crazy, rather there are programmed conditioned minds on autopilot spitting out whatever has been programmed in there.

Anyways... This body/mind mechanism called Björn has a habit of recording videos of blabbering about non-duality. I recorded a video where I was asking all these questions and coming with statements about how paradoxical It all seems and how futile it is even to be asking those questions and recording it.

I then went back again to your email and did some contemplation. Then I watched the video again that I just recorded and it struck me that all this blabbering is just verbal expressions of thoughts arising in awareness. Like there is someone trying and needing to get a definite answer to them. And the very trying and needing to get answers to these thoughts is a step away...they are just something arising in the beingness/awareness, no need to identify with them. Awareness is already always there. It would be like someone trying to find his home through leaving it! Or like you said... knocking on the door to paradise while you are actually IN paradise.

And yet the word awareness IS just a word and concept. Even putting the word "awareness" in place is to distort it. And yet it is not an IT. And even the thought arrising saying "yay – I'm getting somewhere" IS just an arrising thought and to attach to that is also like a step out of true awareness. To think that you are getting somewhere has to be false. There is no one who can get anywhere. It's surely seductive to the mind though because it LOVES being something. It seems even the question "Who am I?", although being a very potent and beneficial question, acting like like caustic soda, IS just a question arising in awareness.

There are thoughts, emotions etc arising that brings back the illusion of an individual self. But it seems effective to ask WHO is thinking this? or WHO is feeling this etc. It seems to "disarm" it all again. An answer is never actually found. But it seems like it's making the very question invalid. Like they are all trick questions.

C: You are getting down to the essence now. Just seeing that ALL of it ... thoughts, emotions, body, mind, is ALL nothing but appearance IN this I AM-ness, your very Being, empty Awareness, or whatever descriptive label we use. This presence-awareness is never OFF, is it? (Except in deep sleep where it appears to be "off" but the evidence that it is NOT "off" is the fact that the body's heart beats, breathing arises etc without no need for a "me" to claim the doing of it.

Keep it real simple, my friend. You are. Being IS. That ... Being ... is a "cognizing emptiness" which you know in the world as "I AM". No one can claim "I am NOT". Being is required and that is what You are.

Make no compromise with That! Speak only from and as the FACT ... Being is a "brute fact" and CANNOT be denied or escaped. Everything else is linguistic imagination, stories or speculations. Or opinions. And the come directly "in tune" with the FACT that "Being IS and I Am That" and refusing to entertain any definition or identification of this Infinite Self that You are is to end the search. Right HERE. RIGHT NOW. You Are That. Before any "thing" is, YOU are. Stay with that and let the Awareness show you the absolute depth of its fullness, and the breadth of its emptiness.

Being is knowing, without the false assumption of a person which you now know in direct practical experience cannot be found. So it boils down to this: There is NO person to attain any state, no special state to attain; the whole thing was a myth; and dispelling the myth is no more complex than getting real about what IS TRUE... knowing the Truth of what you are and refusing any compromise the mind wants to use to paste some imagined limitation onto that Timeless Awareness.

Realizing that the "I" is a CONCEPT with NO ACTUAL reality, and that "time" is ONLY another mental concept, pulls the plug on the illusion once and for good.

Looking directly at what IS from/AS Naked Awareness, seeing directly the Source of the "I Am", the freedom you are comes naturally back to the foreground. And life goes on in effortless joy and there is as Nisargadatta put it, "nothing wrong any more." Seeing that ALL ideas of who or what we are are absolutely FALSE, the deal is done.

So in the end it is as it is before the beginning: You Are Unborn. Absolute freedom. The natural, or Eternal, Being-That-You-Are!

As all the sages have pointed out, it all boils down to knowing what you are as non-conceptual-izable. That keeps it basic and simple.

Good to interact with you my friend.... from I AM to I AM, with Love! Stay in touch as the One moves that and just remember, YOU were never bound, never limited, it was all a myth, believed in innocence and ignorance. Now you know better!

Q (2 Months Later): It has been more than 2 months now since the previous email. Just thought I would send you an update.

What has been happening since then is like dust settling after a whirlwind. Naturally, there was a bit of confusion at first, but now it's all much clearer. What is so striking now is the simplicity of it all.

Before I used to think about what enlightenment was. I was sure it was an advanced and complicated state that could be reached by an individual. All that has all been turned on it's head now. I used to think that so called realized people claiming that the individual self was never true...well these people had actually had an individual self at first and then because of their extensive practices it had been dissolved. But as it is seen now, there REALLY ISN'T any individual self to begin with! That IS the truth...REALLY! That has become so clear. And that has turned many old beliefs on it's head. Even the spiritual ones I was convinced of being true.

Enlightenment as it is usually taught is to me no more than a myth.

Hehe, I used to be angry with so called realized people. Because to me, all they where doing was describing their own state. How they had been dissolved and so on, but that was not helping at all for ME. They couldn't help ME to reach that. Well... no wonder they couldn't... I was not even THERE ! *laughter*

Many things are now the opposite of what was believed before. For example. I used to believe that the so called "state" where there is no identity was a very complicated state. But that is only the natural effortless state. The really complicated state is in fact the state of separation! That state is filled with effort and illusion.

C: This is really beautifully put! Nothing much to add! Now you know that this direct concept-free knowing, the natural statelessness of what is real and forever unchanging, is the home we never left. VERY well done, my friend. Much Love to you!

A few more Thank You Notes

I would like to acknowledge a few people who have had a profound and welcome impact on me. In addition to John Wheeler, to whom this book is dedicated, I offer great thanks and deep appreciation, respect and affection to these dear friends and teachers (in alphabetical prder):

Annette Nibley,

http://www.whatneverchanges.com

Bob Adamson,

http://members.iinet.net.au/~adamson7/index.html

John Greven

http://johngreven.blogspot.com/

and Werner Erhard

http://www.wernererhard.com

Contact Charlie at:

e-mail: non.duality@yahoo.com

telephone: USA +1 580.701.4793

skype: charliehayes36

facebook: charliehayes36

website: www.theeternalstate.org

(blog: beingisknowing.blogspot.com)

"Snail Mail"

1111 S. Oakwood Rd. #1308

Enid, Oklahoma 73703, USA

Feel free to visit but please call first for an appointment.

Made in the USA
Columbia, SC
07 July 2018